Silver Clay
Keepsakes

Katie Baum and Judi L. Hendricks

Silver Clay Keepsakes

FAMILY-FRIENDLY PROJECTS

Katie Baum and Judi L. Hendricks

KALMBACH BOOKS

Kalmbach Books
21027 Crossroads Circle
Waukesha, Wisconsin 53186
www.Kalmbach.com/Books

Please follow appropriate health and safety measures when working with torches and kilns. Some general guidelines are presented in this book, but always read and follow manufacturers' instructions. Every effort has been made to ensure the accuracy of the information presented; however, the publisher is not responsible for any injuries, losses, or other damages that may result from the use of the information in this book.

Published in 2009
13 12 11 10 09   1 2 3 4 5

Manufactured in the United States of America

ISBN: 978-0-87116-285-4

Photos of projects in progress by David Baum. Gallery photos by Robert E. Stotts.

Publisher's Cataloging-in-Publication Data
Baum, Katie.
   Silver clay keepsakes : family friendly projects / Katie Baum and Judi L. Hendricks.

   p. : ill. (chiefly col.) ; cm.

   Includes bibliographical references.
   ISBN: 978-0-87116-285-4

1. Precious metal clay—Handbooks, manuals, etc. 2. Souvenirs (Keepsakes)
3. Silverwork—Handbooks, manuals, etc. I. Hendricks, Judi L. II. Title.

TT213 .B38 2009
739.27

Contents

Introduction

You may have heard about this wonderful "silver clay stuff" that you shape like modeling clay. As instructors in silver clay, we field a lot of questions about what you can do with this stuff. A lot of queries are a little out there (yes, you could create a full-sized pure silver sword if you felt the need), but a lot of them are very down-to-earth: "I want to make a bracelet for my daughter to commemorate my grandson's first steps." Or "What can I make for my parents' 50th wedding anniversary? I want to do something really personal from the whole family." These are the kinds of projects you'll find in this book.

Personalized gifts are where silver clay truly shines. Anyone can buy a platter that says "Happy 50th" in silver leaf. To present one that features the handprints of the couple's own grandchild is not only impossible to buy, but absolutely personal and priceless. Personalization brings an intimacy to the gift that raises it to the level of keepsake.

All of the projects we present are designed with the love and appreciation of family and friends in mind. We hope you'll pour your passion and your creativity into them, just as we have, and that every person who receives one as a gift appreciates the finished work as well as the love with which it was made.

Katie Judi

How to Use This Book

For those of you who have never laid a finger on silver clay before, welcome! This book is designed for you. After you've tried your first few projects, you'll be turning to silver clay as a creative outlet in ways you've never imagined.

You'll find everything you need to know to get started in "Gearing Up," including an introduction to basic materials, tools, and techniques. To become solid silver, the clay needs to be sintered (heated into a solid mass without melting), which requires extreme heat. Many of the projects can be completed with a small butane torch (the kind you'd use to make crème brûlée) or fired on a stovetop. Some projects require a programmable kiln. We identify the firing options at the beginning of each project, so you'll know what's required before you start working.

We have grouped related tools into kits in the next section. You'll use many of these tools constantly as you work with silver clay, so to avoid repetition, we simply call for certain kits at the start of each project. All of the materials and any specialty tools needed are listed as well.

The projects are grouped into three sections. "Simply Silver" projects keep the focus on amazing silver clay. In "Silver Plus," you'll see how silver clay combines beautifully with other elements. "Silver On Ceramics" shows how easy it is to customize ceramic objects by painting on a special form of silver paste.

Silver clay is so user friendly that even young children and teens can participate in making some of the projects. Just read through the instructions to get acquainted with the steps before you get started.

As you page through the projects, you'll find a keepsake to help you celebrate and commemorate nearly every stage of life and love. And you can make every one!

> **Access to a kiln** may be closer than you think. Check with your local bead shops, community college, or paint-it-yourself pottery studio.

4

1 Gearing Up

ABOUT METAL CLAY

Silver clay becomes 99.9% pure silver (fine silver) after firing. Sterling silver is 92.5% silver and 7.5% copper. Fine silver tarnishes much more slowly than sterling, taking on a natural golden, rather than black, patina.

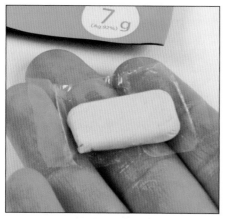

Lump silver clay is available in packages ranging from 7–50 grams.

What is metal clay?

Metal clay is the generic term for clay made with silver, gold, and other metals, designed for use in jewelry, crafts, and art. Metal molecules, water, and a nontoxic, organic binder are combined to make a smooth clay that is kneadable, sculptable, and holds any texture you desire. The high firing heat burns away the binder, leaving a slightly smaller solid silver (or other metal) object.

The amazing result of this invention is that, with very little training, nearly anyone can make heirloom-quality jewelry or commemorative items. And you can do this in the comfort of your own home— even working at the kitchen table.

We just can't say enough about metal clay as a crafting medium. Almost anything you can imagine, you can make with this stuff! We've seen vases, bowls, napkin rings, cups, crowns, candleholders, candle snuffers, tea bag holders, letter openers, salt cellars, goblets, bookmarkers, buttons, beads, bottle stoppers, chopstick rests, hat pins, hair combs, handbag handles, helicopters, toothpicks, minuscule trains on rolling wheels, wee dragons, armadillo paperweights, shoe clips, mezuzahs, menorahs, a miniature silver cornucopia, knives, forks, spoons, trinket boxes, picture frames and, of course, jewelry—in every imaginable shape, size, and color ... and the list goes on.

Clay made from silver is the most commonly used metal clay, and it's used for all the projects in this book. Art Clay Silver and PMC—the two brands of silver clay—become pure silver once they have been fired. (Other metal clays made with bronze and copper have been recently introduced.)

Where to find metal clay

To find a supplier for metal clay, check on the Web or ask whether your local bead store offers classes and supplies. You can also find more information on metal clay organizations and sources on p. 107. Certified metal clay instructors sometimes distribute the product affiliated with their certification or can refer you to a good source.

Different formulas of clay are available. As metal clay has evolved, the product formula has been tweaked to the point that today, you can buy a high-quality version that has a convenient, short firing schedule and minimal shrinkage.

Low-fire silver clay (ACS 650 or PMC3), which is used in many of the projects, can fire at a low temperature (lower than 1300°F/700°C). The beauty of low-fire clay is that you can use a butane torch or a stovetop for firing. It can also be combined with and fired alongside other higher-fire formulas with success. Low-fire clays are also fantastic for use with other materials that don't hold up well in higher temperatures, such as certain gemstones, ceramics, and glass.

Throughout the book, we've tried to simplify your choices as much as possible by recommending that you use low-fire clay wherever possible.

Basic clay types

Different forms of silver clay have different consistencies; the following is an introduction to the most common types you'll use.

Lump clay, the basic form, is sold in a small, resealable pouch by gram weight. It starts out like a flattened ball of dough.

Paste clay, which comes in a small jar, is the consistency of cake batter; it can be painted onto surfaces (such as a leaf, to make a silver leaf from a real leaf) or used to join pieces of unfired clay. It's also helpful for filling seams and cracks.

Syringe clay is slightly stiffer than paste clay; it comes in a syringe dispenser, ready to extrude through a nozzle—like piping frosting onto a cake. It has a texture similar to toothpaste. All Art Clay Silver syringe clay is low-fire, so it can be used with either low-fire or high-fire lump clay. PMC sells syringe clay in different formulas to match its lump clay. Art Clay offers tips in three widths; the PMC syringe tip can be trimmed to the width you like. Most projects call for a medium syringe tip, which creates a line that's just under a millimeter wide (about the diameter of 20-gauge wire).

Paper- or sheet-type clay comes in flat squares that are perfect for making shapes with scrapbooking punches or folding origami-style. This silver clay type can also be quilled (rolled into curlicues) and pasted to other unfired clay pieces.

We don't call for this form in the projects, but it's fun to experiment with.

Overlay Paste, available only in the Art Clay Silver brand, acts as an intermediary layer between any nonporous surface and silver, so it's the product of choice for adding silver surface embellishment to glass or stoneware. We like this technique a lot and devoted an entire chapter of projects to it ("Silver On Ceramic," which begins on p. 81). Overlay Paste is a low-fire material. It can also be used to adhere finished pieces of silver together and to repair fired silver pieces that have been damaged.

As you explore the metal clay world, you'll encounter other forms of silver clay as well as other metal types that aren't used in this book. Read the manufacturer's instructions for each product you use, including those mentioned briefly here. Other great sources of information are the certified teacher or source from which you purchased the clay, the Internet, and the resources listed on p. 107.

Use silver clay paste to join unfired clay, paint onto surfaces, and fill seams.

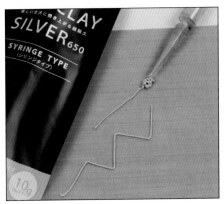

Use syringe clay for capturing stones and adding details like lines and filigree.

TECHNIQUES AND TOOLS

You can learn the basics of working with metal clay in an hour and find the basic tools you need in the average kitchen (although we recommend gathering a kit of dedicated metal clay tools rather than raiding the kitchen drawers!).

Can you roll cookie dough? Then you can roll metal clay. Can you brush barbecue sauce onto grilled food? Then you can use paste to make a silver leaf. If you can stamp your address onto an envelope or use an emery board to file your fingernails, you can texture your clay while it's wet and sand it smooth once it's dry. It really is that easy!

It is this same combination of shaping, texturing, molding, drying, sanding, smoothing, and firing skills that create any and every silver clay keepsake. Whether you use silver by itself or want to combine it with other media, these are the techniques you'll use again and again.

Between uses, store your syringe with the tip down in a small cup of water to prevent the clay from drying out.

Working with wet clay

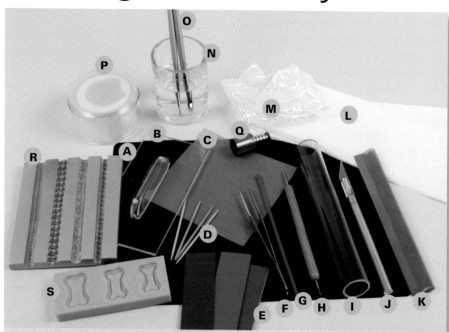

WET-CLAY TOOL KIT

The basics: [A] nonporous work surface, [B] snake roller, [C] nonstick sheet, [D] toothpicks, [E] graduated slats (or playing cards), [F] tweezers, [G] narrow straw, [H] scribing tool, [I] rolling tool, [J] craft knife, [K] tissue blade, [L] paper towels, [M] plastic wrap, [N] cup of water, [O] narrow paintbrushes, [P] olive oil. Some projects will call for specialty tools such as: [Q] clay cutter, [R] mold, and [S] stamp.

As you work, always put extra clay back in the original package or keep it moist (see p. 22). **For a handy oil dispenser,** moisten a small sponge with a bit of oil and keep it in a cup.

Getting started with your clay

Work at a table that's a comfortable height, and protect the table with a **nonporous work surface** such as a thin, flexible cutting mat or a glass cutting board. If your project requires you to cut long lines or measured shapes, you might find a graph mat helpful.

Place a smaller **nonstick surface**, such as Teflex (sold as a baking sheet), over the work surface. This nonstick sheet is semitransparent, so you can place it over a template or the graph mat and still see lines or patterns.

Olive oil, mineral oil, or Badger Balm will help keep the clay from sticking to

your hands or tools. Every time you begin working, use the oil or balm to lightly condition your roller, hands, and any texturing tools.

A very light application is enough; you want just the slightest sheen of oil on your hands and tools. Katie is fond of saying, "If you find yourself fantasizing about a pasta dinner while you work, you've used too much." The oil provides a moisture barrier between the clay and your hands, preventing dry skin from soaking up moisture from the clay. All metal clay begins to dry once it is opened, and the last thing you need is for the clay to dry out even faster!

After opening your metal clay, knead the lump briefly—just enough to start to soften the clay and make it workable.

Rolling is a basic metal clay skill, and you have many options for rolling tools. A clear acrylic **roller** lets you see the shape you're rolling, which is handy if you're aiming for a certain size. Some folks use a short length of narrow PVC pipe. Another option is borrowed from cake decorating—an opaque fondant roller, which comes with rings to control the thickness of the rolled dough (or, in this case, clay). Remember when we mentioned that you can find all the tools you'd need in your average kitchen? You can find some really awesome metal clay accessories in kitchen stores. The cake decorating aisle is a gold mine!

If your roller didn't come with its own measuring tools like the fondant roller, you can use color-coded **graduated slats** (purchased from a metal clay supplier) or **playing cards** to measure the thickness of the clay. Playing cards are cut to a regulation size and thickness; each card is 0.25 mm, so 4 cards equals 1 mm. (You can make handy card stacks by taping sets of cards together and labeling them.) Our project directions give thickness in millimeters as well as number of cards. To roll the clay to a certain thickness, place a slat or card stack on each side of the clay and roll over the top of the cards and the clay.

A **snake roller** is an acrylic sheet (some come with handles) that helps you roll smooth, even snakes or rods of clay. You can use these snakes to make bails, rings, or long tubes.

Sometimes it's just a lot easier to extrude the clay, especially if your piece requires thin snakes. For that, use an **empty silver clay syringe** (don't use the syringe clay itself for snakes; it's not dense enough). Prepare the syringe by drawing up and squirting out water a few times, pack lump clay inside, and depress the plunger to extrude. Another option is to purchase an **extruder** designed for use with metal clay.

Molding and forming

The easiest way to shape your clay is to use a mold, and there are oodles of ways to do this. A very simple route is to use a **purchased mold**. Molds come in all shapes and sizes, from frames to rings to cameos. There are molds for bracelets and molds for shapes. Some molds are made specifically for crafts, but—once again!—the baking aisle holds treasures (think candy and fondant molds).

Of course, there will be times when you're searching for the perfect something and can't quite seem to find it. Or the reverse: You have the perfect something and want to make a replica of it. For this, use a silicone-based, **two-part molding compound**. Combine equal amounts of the two parts until the compound is a uniform color, and then press your item into the mix with even pressure. The compound sets quickly (in five minutes) and makes a flawless relief of any item. Test if the mold is set by pressing your

fingernail into the side; if your fingernail does not make a mark, your mold is ready to use. The mold is flexible and reusable, needing only a little olive oil (or the release agent of your choice).

If you plan to kiln-fire, you can make a form using organic material that will burn away in the kiln (see p. 14 for more information on kiln-firing). One of these materials is **cork clay**, available from metal clay suppliers. Sculpt a shape from cork clay and wrap rolled-out metal clay around it or add layers of silver paste to the shape. Cork clay needs at least 24 hours to dry and must be fired in a kiln without interruption.

Almost anything organic is a candidate for creating a form, because it will burn away in the kiln, leaving the silver shape behind. Want cute little doughnut-shaped beads? Coat Cheerios with silver paste! Cereals make great bead shapes, and they are inexpensive. If you want little round beads, use Kix; square beads, use Cap'n Crunch.

You may be tempted to try using papier-mâché products sold at craft stores to create forms. We've tried it, with unreliable results. Cork clay works far better.

There are plenty of other organic choices for molding and shaping, from deeply veined leaves to wooden ice pop sticks. The items need to be organic—and dry—no plastic, no resins, no craft foam, no wax or waxed papers, no rubber, nothing petroleum-based. Do not try putting a crayon in with your clay to turn it purple. At a minimum, the smell these items create is enough to drive you from the immediate vicinity. On a larger scale, you risk damaging your equipment with residues and chemicals. And by *equipment,* we also mean your lungs, as these foul-smelling chemicals can be toxic. Stick to Cocoa Puffs, OK?

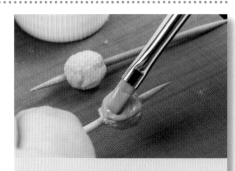

Beads from cereal

Skewer the cereal piece on a toothpick and cover the piece in several layers of paste, until the silver is at least .5 mm thick. Allow each layer to dry thoroughly before applying the next. When dry, remove the piece from the toothpick for firing. The hole you created will allow gases from the burning cereal to escape during firing. If you're making beads, you may want to create two holes for stringing. Whatever the intended use, always remember to create an "escape valve" when coating organic forms like these.

Polymer clay (Fimo and Sculpey are two brands) is inexpensive, and it doesn't dry out as you work with it as metal clay does. It's excellent for practicing rolling, shaping, and sculpting.

Scribing

Judi's trick for scribing a design or words is to print the design or lettering to size, stretch a piece of plastic wrap tightly over the surface of the clay, and trace over the paper. When you lift the paper, you'll have a light indentation in the clay. Retrace the shapes with your scribing tool or a ball-point pen before removing the plastic wrap. The plastic won't stick to the clay, and it helps prevent rough edges in your scribed design.

Texturing

We like texture. Texture makes a huge difference between a bland design and an eye-catching work of art. We are texture collectors ... maybe even texture junkies. Texture can provide the focal point of a silver piece or play a supporting role as a background element.

Texture plates (also called texture mats or sheets) come in many designs and materials. Plastic texture mats are inexpensive and easy to clean; rubber texture sheets are flexible and leave crisp, detailed impressions. You can also use rubber stamps or embossers for texture. If you want to create an original pattern, we show you how to do it using photopolymer plates (see p. 104). A stamp block or even a pencil eraser can be carved into simple shapes.

Condition your texture plates or stamps before use to prevent the clay from sticking. Use a stiff paintbrush to push a bit of olive oil into all the nooks and crannies.

Scribing, smoothing, and cutting

A great perk of silver clay is that every project can be personalized by adding the recipient's name or some other personal design to the piece. One way to do this is by scribing into moist clay, and any pen or tool with a pointy tip such as a needle tool, toothpick, or bamboo skewer works great as a **scribing tool**. Try using a light poking motion—as if you're giving the clay a tattoo—to roughly scribe the lettering or symbols in the clay, and then go back and smooth the impressions. If you drag a tool through the clay, you may cause the clay to pull up on the sides, leaving crusty bits when it dries.

For smoothing seams and reaching into tiny crevices, collect a few inexpensive **paintbrushes** of various bristle lengths, stiffnesses, and shapes. You'll find uses for a variety of brushes ranging from an extra-fine-point liner to a medium-width chisel shape. Keep a dry brush handy for collecting silver dust.

A **craft knife** helps trim clay into any shape, from simply symmetrical to wildly whimsical. For trimming a really straight edge, use a **tissue blade**. For specialty shapes, start a collection of all types and sizes of cookie and fondant cutters, or purchase clay cutters designed for cutting polymer and metal clay shapes.

Attachments

Don't forget to make a way for your piece be worn or displayed! It's so simple: While the clay is moist, use a small **straw** (a cocktail straw or coffee stirrer works great) to punch a hole approximately 2 mm from the edge of the clay. When the clay has been fired, you can add a jump ring to attach the piece to a chain or to another silver component. If you forget to punch a hole in the clay while it's wet or prefer a smaller hole than the one you get with the straw, you can always use a **narrow drill bit** held in a **pin vise** to create the holes you need after the clay dries. (It helps if you mark a starter hole with a needle tool while the clay is still wet.)

Not everyone likes the look of holes and jump rings. If you don't, use **pure silver findings** made specifically for embedding in wet clay, such as screw eyes, which look like little keys. Be sure to use fine (pure) silver findings, because sterling, when heated, will blacken with oxidation (see p. 79). Many metal clay suppliers sell fine silver findings.

To attach a screw eye, embed the notched end right up to the bottom of the eye for a really strong grip. Once fired, a little ring is left at the edge of the clay where you can attach a snap-on bail.

Working with dry clay (*greenware*)

Tools for drying clay

The term we use for clay that is totally dry but not yet fired is *greenware,* a term borrowed from ceramics. (No, the silver clay does not actually turn green.) In this state, the clay is brittle and snaps easily under pressure, so it needs to be handled carefully.

Thoroughly drying metal clay is essential to the sintering process. Clay must be absolutely, completely, totally, unquestionably dry before it can be fired; the term for this state of dryness is **bone dry**. Putting moist clay under a torch is like waiting for a popcorn kernel to explode on your firing brick; steam builds inside the wet clay and bursts through the outer surface. If you're lucky, this makes just a little popped bubble in your silver. If you're unlucky, hot shards of half-fired silver can skitter across the room. Now, our point is not to scare you out of torch-firing—we just want to impress on you how essential it is to dry your piece. We'll show you several dependable ways to dry your clay; it's also pretty simple to test whether your piece is dry.

The easiest, most gentle way to dry clay is to let it sit at room temperature to **air dry**. It's also the easiest way to prevent a piece from curling. Let your piece(s) sit out overnight, and go watch a favorite movie, do some laundry, maybe even get some shopping done. Most thin pieces (2 mm or thinner) will dry completely overnight, provided your home's air has average humidity. If you live where it is really dry all of the time, such as in Nevada or Arizona, you can assume that your average-sized silver clay piece will dry completely in a few hours. Often the problem in these arid regions is keeping the clay moist long enough to finish a project. If you live down in the bayous, where you can shower on a Monday and

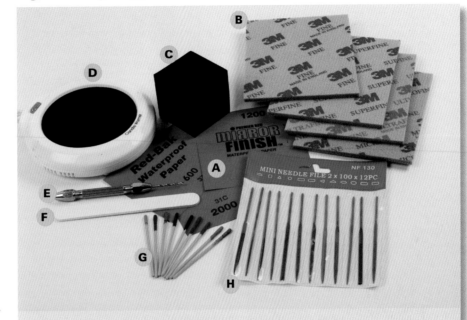

GREENWARE TOOL KIT
The basics: [A] wet/dry sandpaper or [B] sanding pads in coarse to fine grit, [C] rubber block, [D] drying appliance, [E] pin vise, [F] sanding stick, [G] sanding swabs, [H] set of mini files.

your hair will still be wet on Wednesday, you may need a dehydrator to ensure the clay is absolutely dry. If the piece is really thick—⅛ in. (3 mm) or more—always err on the side of caution.

You have choices in **drying appliances**. A **food dehydrator** is a nifty little countertop-sized appliance that dehumidifies, heats, and circulates air within a chamber. These work great for drying metal clay items. You can often find small, inexpensive food dehydrators at resale shops. And although silver clay is nontoxic, please don't share an appliance between food and art. Resign your silver clay dehydrator to a lifetime of foodlessness.

Small drying appliances that can be shared, though, are **hair dryers** and **mug warmers**. Your mug won't care if

> **When sanding greenware,** grasp the work very close to where you are sanding. You're less likely to break your piece that way.

Go MacGyver!

To use a hair dryer without the tedium of holding it, you can rig a homemade dehydrator using a hair dryer and a cardboard box. Cut a hole the size of the dryer nozzle at one end of the box top. Make an exit hole on the opposite side of the box. Put the nozzle in the hole in the top, place your piece inside, and turn the dryer on. Air will circulate through the box and out the opposite hole, drying the clay. Place the clay on a weighted nonstick surface (try refrigerator magnets) so that things don't go flying. We don't advise leaving a MacGyvered dryer unattended.

Snap!

If a clay piece breaks in half before firing, apply a line of syringe clay across the crack, push the pieces back together, let them set for a moment, and smooth the seam with a moist paintbrush. Let dry and sand smooth. No one will ever know the piece was injured!

To test for dryness, put clay on a cool, shiny surface.

Wait 5–10 seconds, slide the piece to the side, and look for condensation. This piece is not yet dry.

a slice of silver has been on the warmer, and this is an effective way to dry clay. Mug warmers get quite hot, nearly 150°F (65°C), so be careful when removing the clay from the surface of the warmer. Sure, it looks like clay—but it's as hot as metal! We recommend keeping the silver on a nonstick surface at all times, so you can lift the piece by the corners of the nonstick paper.

Testing for dryness

So, you ask, how do I tell if clay is dry? We think the truest method is the condensation test. Have you ever breathed on a window to make it fog up? This is the same idea. If you're using a hair dryer, dehydrator, or mug warmer, the clay is heated as it dries, and any moisture left in the piece will condense on a room-temperature surface. Place the clay straight from the drying appliance onto a cool, shiny surface, such as a small mirror. After 5–10 seconds, slide the silver aside. If you see condensation left behind, the piece is not dry. Continue drying until you no longer see any sign of condensation on the glass or metal.

Dry pieces have a slightly chalky feel that still-moist ones don't have (unless they're fairly thick). If you drag a fingernail lightly across a flat section, it feels like a stick of chalk. Another

test that will become second nature is noticing whether the clay feels cool to the touch when it's been sitting at room temperature for a few minutes. Dry clay at room temperature feels neither warm nor cool; wet clay holds moisture that is evaporating, and so it may feel a couple of degrees cooler than room temperature. Until you're very familiar with the clay, continue drying at least 20 minutes past when you think it's dry. Remember that there's absolutely no harm in letting pieces sit overnight or for days until you're ready to fire.

Prefinishing dry clay

You can make any fired silver piece shiny by running it in a tumbler with water and stainless steel shot for two hours. But if you want it to have a true mirror finish, the piece must have all of its lumps and bumps sanded perfectly flat. Although you can sand the piece after it's fired, it's far easier to sand it in the greenware state.

A **rubber block** will be a huge help at this stage, providing a platform so your hands and tools can work all around the edges of the silver. The block helps you reach difficult spots and distributes pressure. At this stage, the dry, porous clay is vulnerable to snapping in half.

To smooth, work from the outside in. Use a **mini file set** or **sanding sticks** (like emery boards) to smooth the edges and remove sharp bits and corners. Generally, if a piece is a little bit sharp before firing, it will be really sharp after firing, and you don't want it to catch on clothing or pinch skin. Once edges are dulled or beveled with the larger tools, use finer sanding materials to further smooth edges, corners, and surfaces. **Sanding swabs** are great for reaching into tiny areas. Katie's favorite sanding tools are 3M **sanding pads** for just about everything, from smoothing to general shaping. 3M also makes **polishing papers**, which work well for delicate surfaces and for preparing greenware for mirror finishing. Sanding silver clay is often the reverse

of what you think it should be. If you want to make a surface level, lay the piece on a broad sanding surface and move the piece in circles. Don't bring the sandpaper to the item; rather, place the item on the sandpaper.

When you're after a shiny, mirror-like finish, sand the silver as smooth as possible with dry sandpaper while it's in the greenware stage. Start with a coarse grit (400 or 600), and sand until all signs of pocking or cracking are gone. Move to a higher grit (1200), and sand until the piece is smooth (you'll notice very little resistance as you move the piece).

Finally, if you want an ultra-smooth finish, use a super-fine grit (2000, available from metal clay suppliers, jewelry suppliers, or an automotive store). You may notice a silvery sheen even before firing.

Hold the sandpaper taut over the rubber block and move the piece in circles.

Sand over a tray or plate so you can reclaim the silver dust; use it to make your own paste (see p. 20).

Firing clay: kiln, torch, and stovetop setups

The firing process brings the clay to sintering temperature. During sintering, the silver molecules become tacky but not fluid; they fuse together in a tight bond without reaching the melting point. The binder in the clay burns away, leaving a slightly smaller solid silver piece.

There are three commonly used ways to sinter metal clay: in a kiln, with a butane torch, or on a gas stovetop. Some projects require a kiln because of specific directions for reaching and holding specific temperatures, such as all of the silver-on-ceramics projects in this book. Some types of clay, such as Original PMC and PMC+, require kiln-firing because they need a high sintering temperature and a long holding time at that temperature. The newest members of the metal clay family, bronze and copper clays, also require a kiln for firing.

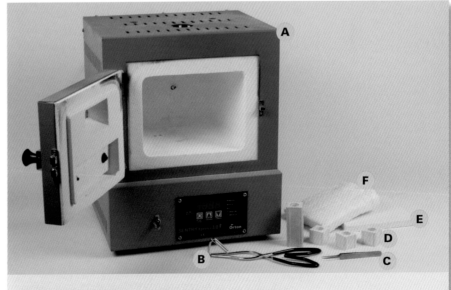

PROGRAMMABLE KILN SETUP
The basics: [A] programmable kiln, [B] tongs, [C] tweezers, [D] kiln posts, [E] ceramic fiber board, [F] fiber blanket.

Kiln safety

Place silver pieces on a ceramic fiber board, which sits on posts in the kiln. Use tongs to move the shelf in and out of the kiln. Usually you will let the kiln cool to room temperature before opening; if you're opening a hot kiln, wear heat-resistant gloves and use filtered safety glasses. If your kiln is in a garage, do not store gasoline near the kiln; the tiniest spark can ignite gas fumes.

Low-fire silver clays (which we use in many projects) are torch- and stove-friendly, sintering happily with the temperature produced by that true, blue flame, held for fairly short periods of time.

You'll find firing schedules and shrinkage rates for a variety of silver clay types on p. 101. To produce the strongest possible silver, fire at the highest recommended temperature for the type of clay you're using for at least the minimum time listed—and there's no harm in firing for a longer period than what's listed.

Kiln-firing

Kiln-firing is pretty simple. We recommend a digitally programmable kiln, which will have built-in programs (and you can program others), so it knows how fast to heat up, what temperature to hold, and for how long. Tabletop, nonprogammable kiln models are available; they won't have the ease of digital programming but are convenient and economical for beginners.

If you don't own a kiln, don't worry, because kiln services are most likely available in your area. Check with local bead shops, glass or ceramic supply stores, and local schools, including colleges and universities. Your silver clay distributor or instructor may offer kiln services or be able to direct you to one. Kiln services are relatively inexpensive, ranging from a per-piece price of several dollars (U.S.) up to about $15 per kiln load for standard firing. Be prepared with specific information and a firing schedule for the type of clay you used, including any special ramping instructions.

When you're ready to purchase your own kiln, check with these same folks about the kiln that best fits your needs. In many cases, they'll be able to set you up with a new or used kiln that suits your needs perfectly. If you become a die-hard silver clay fan (as we believe you'll be), check with local trade shows or conventions you attend. Kilns provided for these events are often sold at a great discount when the conference is over.

Remember, kilns are a *must* for certain projects. Anything that includes glass, large natural gemstones, stoneware or ceramic, or organic material (cork clay, wood, lace, cereals, etc.) needs kiln-firing. Also, any piece heavier than 25 grams or larger than an old-fashioned silver dollar should be kiln-fired.

For glass and ceramics, the kiln provides the temperature control necessary to prevent thermal shock; it's not the actual heat that puts these materials at risk, but rather how quickly they are heated and cooled. Kilns can be set to heat up and cool down (ramp) slowly, controlling the atmosphere around the glass or ceramic item for gentle firing. Torches and stovetops have basically two settings— on and off—which is not as friendly to these materials.

For organic materials, it's a matter of heat versus fire. Organic forms have to be fired in an anaerobic (low-oxygen) environment so that the organic materials smolder slowly at a temperature lower than 1650°F (900°C). If you introduce oxygen, the organic form may burst into flame, briefly raising the temperature above the silver's melting point and ruining the project.

Torch and stovetop safety

Although firing with a torch and on a gas stovetop are wonderfully easy, some people like to see these techniques demonstrated by a teacher. We highly recommend taking an introductory metal clay class if you're timid about playing with fire.

For safety, be sure to tie long hair back. In the average, well-ventilated house, ventilation is seldom a problem. Firing silver clay creates no more smoke or carbon dioxide than a blown-out candle, and won't set off smoke alarms. Just to be on the safe side, though, when firing on the stovetop or with a torch (or if using a kiln indoors), it doesn't hurt to run the vent fan on your range hood.

Torch-firing

First, make sure the clay formula you're using can be torch-fired. Check the chart on p. 101 and review the manufacturer's instructions included with the clay.

Be sure you have a **butane kitchen torch**. Do not use a propane torch or a welding torch—they far exceed the needed temperature and will melt your silver into a small blob within seconds, ruining your hard work. Low-fire silver clay needs a mere 1200°F (650°C) to sinter. Although butane torches can get incredibly hot (up to 2500°F/1370°C), they are small, designed for in-house use, and incredibly easy to control, allowing you to maintain the proper temperature for sintering silver.

Always torch-fire a piece on a **firing brick**, a specially formed refractory ceramic brick that absorbs heat so well that it takes over 15 minutes of firing on the top before the bottom even begins to feel warm. We recommend that your torch has a safety release with a separate ignition switch, a hands-free option, and a way to control the flame size.

Using your dominant hand, release the safety, ignite the torch, and set it for hands-free operation. Hold the torch at a 45-degree angle, and let the tip of the flame lick the silver. Keep the torch moving in slow circles around the piece.

The following signs will let you know where you are in the firing process. First, the piece will seem to ignite, which is the organic binder burning off. This little flash is over quickly; sometimes it's barely noticeable and leaves a faint scent of burning leaves as the binder combusts. Next, the silver seems to turn very white. On a flat piece, you may see the corners pull up a bit (they relax after

a few seconds). Look for a peachy-orange or salmon glow. (You may want to fire in a slightly darkened room so that you can see the color more easily.) When the silver is gently glowing, you'll start timing.

For low-fire clay, the length of time you'll hold at the salmon glow to sinter the silver will depend on the size of the piece; the hold time ranges from 2–5 minutes (see chart). You can't over-fire a piece, so there's no harm in holding for a minute or more past the suggested time. Just keep the piece at the sintering temperature and don't let it get too hot.

Danger, Will Robinson!

If the piece starts looking bright orange, red, shiny, or bubbly, back the flame off. You don't want to melt and liquefy your hard work. Don't shut the torch down; just move the flame a little farther away, continue moving the flame around the piece, and let the silver return to its happy salmon color for the remainder of the hold time.

The fired piece will stay hot for quite a while; move it with **tweezers** or be sure it has cooled completely before touching.

Embrace the blob

If you're still skittish about torch-firing your first beautiful silver clay project, we recommend that you take a small piece of dry clay and deliberately overheat it so that it melts into a blob. Once you've seen with your own eyes what silver looks like as it passes through the sintering temperature to the melting point, you'll never forget it. (And it's kind of fun!)

TORCH-FIRING SETUP
[A] butane torch, [B] firing brick, [C] tweezers.

The piece will seem to ignite at first; this is the organic binder burning off.

Torch and stovetop hold times for low-fire silver clay

Piece size	Hold time
Tiny (5–10 grams)	2 minutes
Small (10–15 grams)	2–3 minutes
Medium (15–20 grams)	3–4 minutes
Large (20–25 grams)	5 minutes

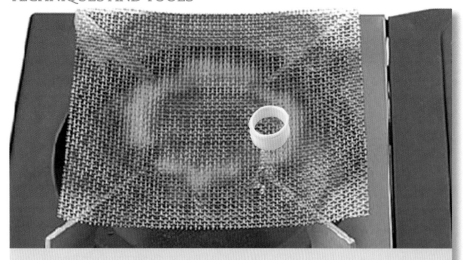

STOVETOP-FIRING SETUP

Fire the piece in the gas burner's hot spot on a stainless steel mesh square. Let the piece cool completely or use tweezers to move it.

Firing review

What can't be fired with a torch or on a stovetop? Organic forms, glass, ceramics, large gemstones, and pieces larger than 25 grams (larger than a silver dollar) must be kiln-fired. Pieces that make great torch- or stove-firing subjects are less than 25 grams of silver, have no organic matter, and contain only small fireable gemstones like CZs (see p. 102 for more on CZs). If something is not kiln friendly, it's definitely not torch friendly. Stay away from plastics, rubber, and craft foam. Fine silver findings that are meant to be embedded, like screw eyes, gem settings, or bail backs, are perfectly fireable using any of the three methods.

Stovetop-firing

Stovetop-firing is very similar to torch-firing. A gas stovetop is necessary; electric coil burners do not generate the heat needed by the silver. Be sure the silver clay formula you're using can be fired in this way (see p. 101), and tie long hair back.

Place a square of **stainless steel mesh** across the stove burner. Turn on the stove and allow the fire to heat the mesh, noting which area becomes red-hot first. This is the hottest part of the flame, which is where you'll place your silver piece. Turn the fire off (for safety), let the mesh cool, and then add your piece to the setup. Turn the burner on again, adjusting the gas flow to the same heat as before. Keep a close eye on the silver, because it's a little harder to see the binder burning away on the stovetop than under a torch.

When the piece begins to glow, start timing while keeping a close watch on the silver. Use the chart on p. 15 to determine the hold time for low-fire clay pieces. If the piece begins to glow a vibrant orange or red, turn the fire down but not off. Adjust the flame to keep the piece at the nice, salmon glow for the recommended time. (Luckily, very few stovetops get hot enough to heat silver to cherry red.)

If your piece isn't 100% dry, the expanding moisture may cause it to pop as it's heated. For safety, you can lay a second piece of mesh lightly on top of the piece, or fire on the back burner so that if the piece pops, it will land on the stovetop.

Quenching/crash-cooling

We like silver clay because of its ability to provide instant gratification. We can make a pure silver pendant, dry it, and fire it within an hour. What a surprise, then, that you can also rush the cooling of a piece. Just as with drying, you can always leave well enough alone and let any piece cool down where it sits—in the kiln, on the firing brick, or on the stove grate. But if you just can't wait, you can quench, or crash-cool, which means you quickly cool a fired piece by placing it in a dish of cool water.

To prepare for quenching, fill a small stainless steel bowl with cool water (never use a glass or paper or foam cup). It's best not to drop flame-red silver directly into the water; let it cool on the firebrick or stovetop grate a minute or so first. The silver will still be very hot, so grasp it carefully with a pair of sturdy tweezers (self-locking tweezers are great) and dip it into the bowl. You may hear a hiss after you submerge the piece—that's normal.

What can you crash-cool? If the piece is all silver, it's safe to quench. Never quench glass, ceramics, or anything that has a gemstone of any sort—natural or CZ.

Solid silver items are perfect candidates for quenching (crash-cooling) in water.

Finishing after firing

You'll have a few options when it comes to finishing your silver, from a matte finish all the way to a mirror-bright finish.

Silver looks white immediately after firing due to the arrangement of the silver molecules on the surface of the fired clay. Brushing a piece with a **stainless steel or brass brush** will create a matte, brushed-nickel appearance. Some people like to brush the piece under running water or in a shallow dish of water, although brushing can be done dry as well.

Use an **agate burnisher** and some elbow grease to shine up your silver. Agate is a natural stone that's just slightly harder than silver. The agate burnisher compresses the silver, giving it a high luster without damaging it. To burnish, place the broadest area of the blade against the silver and move in circles while applying pressure. (Metal burnishers may work, but they are harder than agate and can leave unattractive gouges in the silver if not used carefully.)

To get a shiny finish with very little labor, invest in a **rotary tumbler**. Just drop your silver pieces in the barrel for a couple of hours along with stainless steel shot, burnishing compound, and water.

FINISHING TOOL KIT
The basics: [A] stainless steel or brass brushes, [B] agate burnisher, [C] toothbrush, [D] polishing pads or [E] wet-dry sandpaper from 600–2000 grit, [F] jewelry-grade silver polish, [G] polishing cloth, [H] baking soda. Optional (for patina): [I] liver of sulfur, cotton swab.

Burnishers and tumblers shine silver nicely, but we believe the best mirror finishes are created by hand with abrasives—**wet-dry sandpaper** or **polishing pads**. Keep separate sets of abrasive media—one for fired silver and one for greenware.

Mirror finishing
Here's our process for getting a mirror finish by hand: You can skip the brushing step. Begin with 600-grit wet-dry

To add patina to the entire item, hang it from a paper clip or twist tie and dip it in the liver of sulfur solution.

sandpaper (substitute polishing pads here if you prefer). Work under running water or in a shallow bowl of water. Wet the fired piece and the sandpaper thoroughly, and sand until your fingers are numb. (We admit: Mirror-finishing by hand is somewhat grueling, and is another technique that might be easier to learn from an instructor. We find it noticeably more attractive than tumbling or burnishing. If you have the time and energy, it's well worth the elbow grease. You'll experience a warm buzz of accomplishment from taking an uneven surface and making it mirror smooth.)

Examine the silver closely; don't be afraid to use a magnifying glass or visor. Sand with wet 600 grit until you see no pocking, unevenness, or scratches. Rinse the piece and change the water if you've been using a bowl. Repeat this process with 1200 grit, then again with 2000 grit. At an amazingly smooth 2000 grit, you should notice a nice sheen on the metal. If you're a perfectionist, feel free to keep going up to higher grits—they make sanding pads up to 12,000 grit—but 2000 is usually high enough if you also took time to smooth the surface at the greenware stage.

Use a **jewelry-grade silver polish** to add a final shine and protect from tarnishing if you don't plan to add a patina to your silver (polishing will remove patina). Put a teensy bit of polish (a half-pea size for approximately 15 grams of finished silver) on a soft polishing cloth and rub hard onto the silver. If you've finished this piece by hand, take a minute or five to admire your work, because the moment right after you've finished polishing is when you realize that it was worth all of the effort. We also suggest that you carry your piece around the house and make everyone you can find check it out, too.

Adding patina to fired pieces

Many people like the look of a colored or dark patina on their silver pieces—it's great for emphasizing texture and lettering. The most common way to add patina to silver is by using liver of sulfur (often abbreviated to LOS) solution, a stinky (like rotten eggs) concoction that creates a beautiful rainbow of coloration across the surface of silver. LOS is available as dry chunks or in liquid form, and it can produce extraordinary results … as long as you're willing to embrace its unpredictable nature.

Make sure you have good ventilation when using LOS. Clean your silver thoroughly in a paste of **baking soda** and water, brushing with a **soft brush** (a toothbrush is fine) to remove oils from the surface. Rinse well in clean water. To prepare the patina solution, mix about a cup of almost-boiling water with a chunk of liver of sulfur the size of a fingernail until the chunk dissolves. The stronger the patina solution, the quicker the silver will take the color. Heat intensifies the reaction; rinsing in hot tap water will darken the color. You will also need clear rinsing water, either in a small bowl or from a running tap.

If you want to color the entire piece, front and back, use a dipping tool to keep your hands out of the sulfurous solution. A reshaped paper clip or twist tie works well. Hook the wire onto the piece, and dip the piece into the solution. Raise the piece quickly to peek at it. The solution will continue to color the silver even if the silver is not submerged. If you want to continue the coloration, dip the piece again, raise it, and check the progress. As soon as you see color you like, rinse the piece thoroughly in cold rinse water to stop the chemical process.

For coloring small areas, dip a cotton swab into the LOS solution and paint it on the surface.

There are many tips, tricks, and suggestions for how to get the best color from your LOS. Some people use ice-cold rinse water; others use boiling hot rinse water. We use hot water for rinsing and think that it helps us keep brighter blues and purples on our silver.

To neutralize the solution, leave it near a sunny window in a clear container for a day or so until it loses its yellow color.

Final touches

You can remove some of the patina from the high points of your design with a polishing pad or cloth, leaving dark accents in the recesses. Don't rub or polish the silver too much or you'll remove the patina you just added.

As the silver tarnishes over time, the patina you created will oxidize and change. You can either allow this to happen and buff off and reapply the patina, or you can apply a thin coat of lacquer to seal the surface. Try a lacquer used on brass instruments (such as Staybrite), a high-gloss lacquer made for use on metals (found at hardware stores), or a microcrystalline wax like Renaissance.

Bottom line, LOS is a bit unpredictable, more than a little stinky, and makes for a great deal of fun experimentation. Many projects in this book suggest adding patina. Try a different approach for each!

Assembling finished work

A project is not truly completed until it has been fully put together, ready to enjoy. This means that a pendant has a jump ring or a bail and is on a chain. Charms are attached to bracelets. Bracelet links have been connected with jump rings. Good tools and the proper techniques will help you do this well.

Use two pairs of pliers to work with jump rings—two pairs of chainnose pliers or one chainnose and one flatnose. Buy jewelry-making pliers (don't raid the household toolbox!). You need smooth-jawed pliers that won't mar the jump rings.

To open jump rings, grab an end with each pair of pliers and push one end away while you move the other one toward you. Move them so they open as if they were part of a larger coil of rings (which they once were!). Opening rings in this way preserves their circular shape, and all you need to do to close them is reverse the motion so that the ends meet up again.

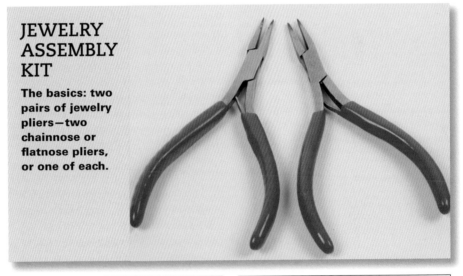

JEWELRY ASSEMBLY KIT

The basics: two pairs of jewelry pliers—two chainnose or flatnose pliers, or one of each.

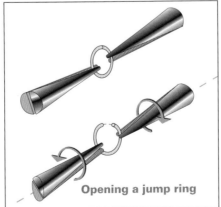

Opening a jump ring

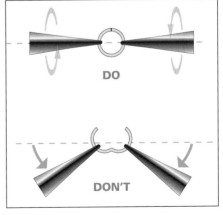

DO

DON'T

Clay care and recycling

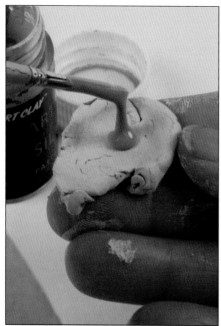

Add silver clay paste to clay that's starting to dry out. Squeeze the lump clay between your fingers to blend and reconstitute the clay.

Silver clay is not an inexpensive material to work with. Caring for your clay will help you stretch your investment. Silver clay is a great lesson on recycling, as you can save all your bits and dust and turn it back into viable clay. Remember that metal clay is always usable, no matter how moist, dry, new, or old it is. Also, how you treat your clay before, during, and after you've begun a project affects how the clay performs during the creation process.

Recycling and reusing: stretching your silver

During the process of making silver items, we create all sorts of silver dust and chunks that cover our work area. Whenever you punch a hole, you remove a little niblet of clay with the straw. Whenever you drill with a pin vise, you remove little curlicues of clay. When you file and sand greenware, you take off a fine layer of clay that falls to your work surface as silver dust.

This precious dust is not something you want to literally blow away. Use a **dry, stiff paintbrush** or **stencil brush** to gently sweep the extra silver dust out of the nooks and crannies of your piece and onto your work surface (a piece of nonstick sheet is great for collecting the dust). Luckily, the silver clay creates a heavy dust, and it will settle to your work surface quickly. Resist the urge to hold up your piece and blow on it.

Your puff of breath does two things, neither of them good: You send silver dust into the air, where you could inhale it into your lungs (bad), and you also lose money in the form of reclaimable silver floating in the breeze (also bad). The silver, while nontoxic if swallowed, is not meant to be inhaled.

Keep a jar of silver paste (we call it the "paste pot") on the work table at all times for reclaiming all of the dust and silver bits that you brush off your pieces. With a little water and some steady stirring, you can create your own paste. If you use different formulas of clay, make separate paste pots for each. For example, adding high-fire dust to low-fire paste changes the characteristics of the paste altogether, requiring the resulting piece to be fired at a higher temperature. *When in doubt, fire at the higher firing temperature for the longer period of time.* Remember, all silver clay can be fired at the higher temperatures— but do not exceed 1650°F (900°C) or the silver will begin to melt.

Overlay Paste considerations

There's no real problem with mixing brushes and water with most silver clay products. Your paste and syringe clays are made to blend with lump clay, so using a brush to apply paste, then to smooth syringe clay, creates no problem.

ACS Overlay Paste is a different story. Because Overlay Paste is formulated to bond to ceramic, glass, and metal, it's best to keep a set of tools that you use only with this formula to ensure the bonding ability of this product. Judi has a set of paintbrushes, water jars for resting those brushes, files, and sandpaper she uses *only* with Overlay Paste. It's a good idea to work with this product from a secondary palette (the jar lid is handy) rather than working straight from the jar.

Contamination during sanding

As you choose your sandpaper and sanding pads, be sure to select fine-grit papers that are designed for jewelry use. If you use coarse-grit papers to remove material quickly, you risk transferring the sanding grit to your new piece and to the silver dust you collect for reuse. Dispose of the sanding surface or reserve it for use in post-firing finishing. (For these reasons, when doing initial sanding, a mini file can be a better option than gritty sandpaper.)

As you sand, any loose sanding grit will blend with your silver dust and get mixed into your paste jar. You might not notice the sanding grit as you use the paste; it's only *after* firing that the grit appears to mar your finish. This is because the silver shrinks, and the minute bits of sanding grit embedded in underlayers pop to the surface.

When we suspect that our paste has been contaminated with sandpaper grit, we reserve its use only for adding paste to the interior of our pieces where imperfections won't show.

In post-firing finishing, none of this matters; you're sanding metal and you won't be recycling any dust into a paste jar. Any wet-dry sandpaper (the kind you can use either moist or dry) is fine for post-firing work.

Reconstituting dry clay
Metal clay begins to dry out as soon as the package is opened. We'll share some of the tricks for keeping clay workable. One of the beauties of silver clay is that it is almost always fixable.

If the clay comes out of the package too dry to work with, it's usually because it has been sitting on a shelf too long. Packaged silver clay has a shelf life of approximately 9–12 months. This doesn't mean that older clay is unusable, only that it is more likely to be dry. Learn how to make the best of the situation, and know that your silver is fine and dandy, if a little parched.

If the clay is cracking on the outside but still moist in the middle, try to reconstitute the clay back into moist lump clay. Add paste, a little at a time, to the dry clay. Allow a moment or two for the moist paste to absorb into the lump, then massage the clay in your fingers until it's smooth and workable. The clay may get tacky and stick to your fingers, but it will return to its happy, malleable self in no time.

Make sure you rub the dried clay off your fingers over a work surface to reclaim that dust. You can also use the *finger bowl* method of clay reclamation: Keep a small cup of water at your work area for rinsing your fingertips. After the water is so full of clay that it starts to feel slippery, put it aside to let the water evaporate. It make take a few days, but once the water is reduced, you'll have silver paste.

If the clay is bone dry from the package, it's easier to turn the clay into paste than into lump clay. Grind the clay to powder or to the smallest bits you can, then add it to the appropriate paste pot.

The second method for reconstituting bone-dry clay into paste is Judi's favorite. Drop the dried lump of clay into an empty paste jar and fill it half full of water. Let it sit for a few days, stir it with a bamboo skewer, and let it sit again. It takes two or three days for it to dissolve completely, but it works. If the clay seems too moist, let it sit uncovered until it reaches a workable consistency.

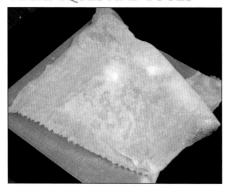

Our Paper-Towel Method for Keeping Clay Moist While Working: Cover with a juicy-wet paper towel.

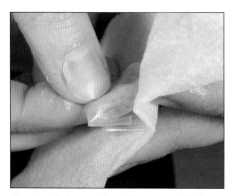

To store leftover clay: Wrap a small piece of plastic wrap around the clay, enclose it in a moist paper towel, and ...

... seal it in the original package. Moisten the towel once a month or so.

If you're determined to make lump clay from this arid bit, you'll need nonstick parchment paper and a thick zip-top plastic bag. Break the parched piece into tiny chunks and place them into a folded pocket of the nonstick surface. Add a few drops of water, and seal the bag. Allow the clay to sit and absorb the water overnight. By morning, you'll have gooey clay in the nonstick pocket.

Massage the clay, keeping it between layers of nonstick surface. Repeat the add-water-and-massage process until the clay is workable and peels easily from the nonstick surface. This process can take several days and can be frustrating, but it does work and the clay is perfectly usable.

You can control the moisture content of the clay as you work with it. As you work with the clay, your first sign that it is drying out is a crackly appearance (like elephant skin, as we once heard it described). You can wipe the clay with a wet paintbrush, smoothing the surface. If the clay has not been shaped, add a drop of water and massage the clay, then start the shaping process. Or keep a travel-sized spray bottle on hand, and spritz the clay with water when it starts to dry.

As you might expect, we have a recommendation: the Paper Towel Method. Keep a juicy-wet, but not drippy, paper towel near your work space. Any time you are not working with the clay, cover it with the wet towel. If the clay starts to get a little dry, cover it loosely with the wet paper towel for a few moments. The paper towel creates a super-humidified environment for the clay, allowing it to absorb moisture without getting sticky at the surface.

Likewise, if you need to walk away from your project for just a few minutes—to answer the phone, take a restroom break, or keep a young child from burning the house down—put the wet towel over your project. Your clay simply can't dry out if it's under a piece of wet paper towel. Katie keeps a timer at her work station. Whenever she walks away from clay, she covers it with a wet paper towel and sets the timer for 7 minutes. If she forgets about her clay, the timer's beep reminds her to come finish her project before it dries out.

Until next time: storing clay

If you are rudely interrupted and cannot finish your project or if you have leftover clay, how you store the clay will determine how often you will need to resort to our reconstituting methods described earlier. The little plastic jars sold for clay keeping are good for short-term storage, but shouldn't be used to keep clay moist for long periods (for more than a week).

Our suggestion? Don't ever throw your silver clay package away! It's nice, heavy plastic and has a resealable, zipper-lock top. Take the extra lump of clay and wrap it inside a square of plastic wrap. Wrap the plastic-covered clay in a wet—but not dripping—paper towel and place it in the original package. Rehydrate the towel once a month or so.

If you don't touch the wrapped clay for a month or so, the paper towel may grow mold. While this is gross, it doesn't affect the quality of the clay—your clay is fine. Just switch out the old wet towel for a new one, wrap the clay, and reseal the package.

2 Simply Silver

Uh-Oh, Fingerprints!
charm or pendant

This project turns your toddler's natural affinity for leaving her or his mark everywhere into something to treasure.

A single fingerprint makes a sweet and meaningful pendant or charm. A few fingerprints can team up for a creative, unique pendant-and-earring set. A fingerprint from each finger (or from each child) can turn into a lovely charm bracelet, with the name of each contributor on the back of each print. Or skip the hanging hole and add a dot of epoxy to the back to attach charms to magnets or photo frames.

quick reference

MATERIALS & TOOLS
1 relatively rested, curious child
  with clean fingers
7 grams low-fire silver clay
  (ACS Slow Dry recommended)
Small oval cutter (optional)
Magnifying glass (optional)

TOOL KITS
Wet-clay tool kit
Greenware tool kit
Finishing tool kit
Jewelry assembly kit

Firing Schedule LOW-FIRE
Butane torch, gas stovetop, or kiln

1 Roll the clay to 1.5 mm/6 cards thick: Center it on the nonstick surface between the measuring slats or playing cards and roll a round pancake shape **[A]**. Be sure to keep the ends of your roller on the slats or cards to prevent the clay from being rolled too thin.

2 Bring on the fingerprints! Lightly condition the toddler's fingertip to ensure a clean release for the fingerprint. Press the finger gently but firmly into the clay, rolling it once in a side-to-side motion **[B]**.

3 Check to make sure that the print is cleanly captured in the clay. (To do this, use the magnifying glass or get close to the print by picking up the nonstick surface.) Rotate the clay to see the contrast in the fingerprint ridges. If the ridges aren't easy to see, ball up the clay and repeat steps 1–2 until you have a great print.

4 Use either the craft knife or the oval cutter to cut around the fingerprint, leaving extra space above the print for a hanging hole. Use a straw to punch a hole above the fingerprint, leaving at least 2–3 mm between the hole and the edge of the clay **[C]**. Dry completely.

Pinch the tidbit of clay out of the straw and add it to the rest of the leftover clay. Wrap the leftover clay in plastic wrap, place it in a piece of moist paper towel, and return it to the original package.

If pressing a finger into the clay isn't working well, try having the child squeeze a little ball of clay between a finger and thumb.

Oh no! My clay is getting dry!

Because you'll be working with an "assistant" in this project and even slow-dry clay begins to dry the moment you open it, preparation is especially important. Let's review: Have all of your materials ready within arm's reach. Lightly condition your roller and hands. Dip a paper towel in water and get it squishy-wet but not dripping; lightly cover your clay with it if you need to step away from your clay for a moment or two.

If your clay starts to feel dry or look crumbly, add a drop or two of plain water to the clay and massage the lump of clay until the water is equally absorbed and the clay is moist enough to use. Don't overwater the clay—too much water leads to silver slush. Knead the clay until it's moist but not slimy and sticky, and move on with your project.

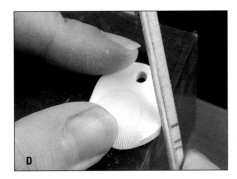

5 Place the piece on the rubber block and gently smooth the edges using files or sanding materials, being careful to avoid the fingerprint [**D**]. Flip the piece over to smooth the edges from the back.

6 Smooth the back of the piece using a progression of sandpapers or sanding pads. Smooth the front of the piece carefully, staying clear of the fingerprint [**E**].

7 Fire the piece according to the low-fire schedule. Because this piece is smaller than 25 grams, it can be torch-fired or fired on a gas stovetop. Allow the piece to cool.

8 Brush with a stainless steel or brass brush for a matte finish [**F**].

9 Use liver of sulfur to add a dark patina, if desired. Apply jewelry polish with a polishing cloth to shine the front and back and bring out the texture of the fingerprint.

10 Attach a jump ring or an earring wire to the charm.

A double-sided pendant can keep the print hidden and close to the heart, if the wearer chooses.

Tiny, dainty, pure-silver fingerprints represent something special, capturing childrens' innocence, individuality, and promise. No two fingerprints are exactly alike, and every silver fingerprint charm is distinct and lovely.

A Good Impression
personalized charms

An outstanding feature of silver clay is its ability to capture textures and images. This project is quite simple to do and easy to adapt into an attractive pendant, charm, or set of earrings. Work with any stamp or texture you choose to show off the style and taste of the wearer.

You may enjoy taking this project a few steps further. Small stamps and cutters will help you create charms for a charm bracelet or a set of earrings. Instead of using a stamp, try impressing your favorite texture or a nice, deeply veined leaf. Nearly any small, raised design will work!

quick reference

MATERIALS & TOOLS
10 grams low-fire silver clay
Stamp or texture mat
Small oval or circle cutter, slightly
  larger than stamp (optional)
Jump ring

TOOL KITS
Wet-clay tool kit
Greenware tool kit
Finishing tool kit
Jewelry assembly kit

Firing Schedule LOW-FIRE
Butane torch, gas stovetop, or kiln

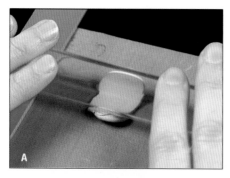

1 Roll 10 grams of clay into a pancake shape to 1.5 mm/6 cards thick **[A]**. (If you will be pressing the clay onto a larger object to capture a texture, roll the clay to 2 mm.)

2 Place the stamp or texture mat in the center of the rolled clay. Press firmly and evenly on the stamp, impressing the image evenly into the clay **[B]**. Use gentle pressure; don't press so hard that you break through the clay to the work surface. Lift the stamp straight up from the clay. If you're using a texture mat, use the roller to press the texture evenly into the clay, and peel the mat gently off the clay.

For the best impression, don't wiggle the stamp. If you're rolling a texture mat, don't rock the roller back and forth. Side-to-side motion tends to create a funky, distorted image.

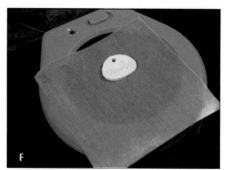

3 Using a narrow straw, punch a hole above the impression **[C]**.

4 Use a craft knife **[D]** or a small cutter **[E]** to trim the clay around the impression. Store excess clay for another project.

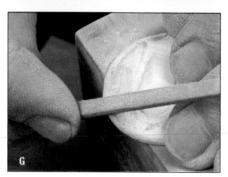

5 Dry the piece thoroughly **[F]**.

6 Remove any sharp edges from the piece using a mini file **[G]**, an emery board, or a sanding stick.

7 Sand the front and back of the piece as smooth as possible, avoiding the impression, with sandpapers, polishing papers, or sanding pads [H]. Progress from low to high grit. Create a comfortable, rounded edge on the piece. Remove any dust from the piece with a dry paintbrush, paying special attention to the impressed areas.

8 Fire the piece according to the low-fire schedule using a kiln, kitchen torch [I], or gas stovetop. Because the piece is solid silver, it can be quenched.

9 Brush the piece with a stainless steel or brass brush [J].

10 For a shinier finish, hand polish, tumble, or burnish it [K].

11 Use liver of sulfur to accentuate the texture [L]. Apply jewelry polish with a soft polishing cloth to shine the front and bring out contrast.

12 Attach a jump ring to the hole in the piece and finish into jewelry as desired.

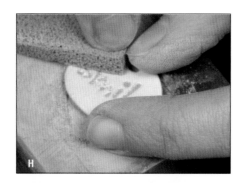

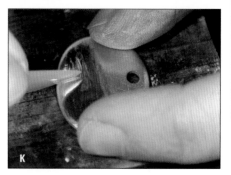

Charm party

This project is well-suited for children ages 7 and above, with an adult to handle the firing. Make it a party! Have an assortment of small stamps available. Small charms each use 3–4 grams of silver. Everyone can enjoy making a charm, an adult fires them, and all the kids enjoy polishing up their work. Consider doing a charm trade; each child could go home with a charm bracelet that you assemble—a combined gift from friends.

Some texture mats offer many design options in one sheet!

For a splash of color, add resin gel after firing (see p. 106).

Sir, Yes Sir!
"dog tag" pendant

The dog tag has been a basic means of identification in the military for generations. In recent years, these tags have become a fashion statement, announcing anything from a favorite sports team to religious affiliation. A trend among teens is to create tags for their significant others, expressing their commitment and feelings.

The dog tag has moved beyond function to decoration and declaration. Now, with silver clay, you can create the perfect message for the perfect gift, featuring any style and statement.

quick reference

MATERIALS & TOOLS
20 grams low-fire silver clay
Card stock or cardboard scrap
Pencil
Scissors
Mini typesetting stamp set or
   other letter stamps
Jump ring

TOOL KITS
Wet-clay tool kit
Greenware tool kit
Finishing tool kit
Jewelry assembly kit

Firing Schedule LOW-FIRE
Butane torch, gas stovetop, or kiln

1 If you are using a typesetting stamp, set up the words or phrases you plan to use.

2 Using the pattern provided as a guide, trace the dog tag shape onto card stock or cardboard. Cut out the shape to make a template.

3 Roll all the clay to 1.5 mm/6 cards thick, making a rectangle large enough to hold the template **[A]**.

4 With the craft knife, trim the clay around the template shape **[B]**. Remove and store excess clay.

5 Punch a hanging hole in one end of the tag using a narrow straw **[C]**. Place the hole at least 2 mm away from the edge of the tag.

6 Using firm, even pressure, stamp the letters or words into the clay **[D]**. For crisp results, don't rock the stamp.

7 Allow the tag to dry completely. Because it's broad and flat, this piece may warp as it dries. The best way to avoid warping is to let the tag dry slowly at room temperature. If you use a drying appliance, flip the tag over often, so the clay doesn't have the chance to curl. Another option: Dry the tag halfway with an appliance, flip the piece over, place a rubber block on it, and finish drying.

8 Smooth the edges of the tag using sanding sticks or mini files **[E]**.

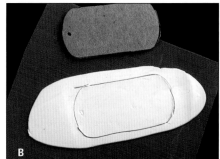

We designed this pattern to allow for some shrinkage. Your fired silver tag will be about 8–12% smaller than the pattern, depending on the type of low-fire clay you use.

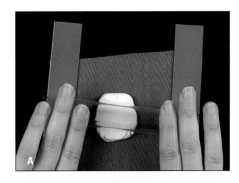

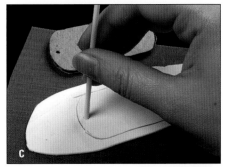

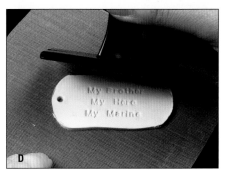

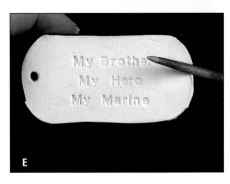

Sometimes the stamp leaves small indentations on the clay, making it look as though the tag was struck with a metal die. If you like that look, which mimics an authentic dog tag, don't smooth the indentations away.

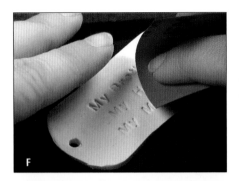

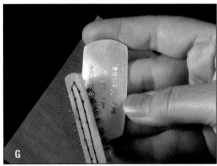

9 Sand the top and back of the tag **[F]**. Depending on your preference for finishing, you can continue smoothing with a progression of finer grits. Brush off and collect any silver clay powder, saving it to be reconstituted into paste.

10 Fire the piece following the low-fire schedule. The piece may warp during firing. The best way to prevent this is to kiln-fire the tag with extra weight on top: Place the tag on fiber board and cover it with fiber blanket and another piece of fiber board. Because the tag is all silver, you can quench it in water for quick cooling after firing.

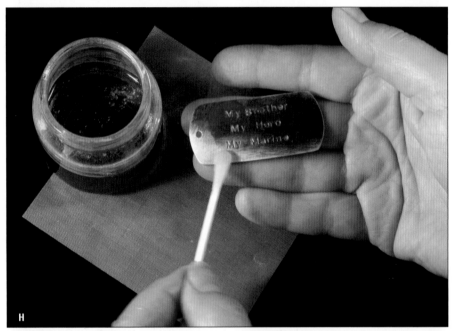

11 Brush the silver with a brass or stainless steel brush **[G]**. This project really pops with a mirror finish. To get that shine, tumble-polish the tag or use an agate burnisher or wet/dry sandpaper.

12 Add patina with liver of sulfur to accentuate the lettering **[H]**.

13 Apply silver polish with a soft polishing cloth **[I]**. As you polish, you'll remove the patina from the raised surfaces, leaving crisp, dark lettering.

14 Attach a jump ring to the tag **[J]**.

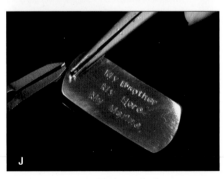

Good Sport

personalized athletic pendant

Being part of a sports team teaches discipline, helps kids learn to work with others, and provides a great outlet for extra energy. It's important to support those who participate, from the kids right on up to their coaches. If your team ends up as regional champion, what better celebration than letting the kids create their own commemorative team pendants?

This project has many options. You can create a shape that has texture like our basketball, either from a texture mat or the actual ball. Other ideas include a baseball, a boxing glove, or a sports jersey, which look beautiful polished to a smooth, mirror finish.

quick reference

MATERIALS & TOOLS
10 grams low-fire silver clay
Circle cutter (optional)
Texture mat or ball (optional)
Jump ring

TOOL KITS
Wet-clay tool kit
Greenware tool kit
Finishing tool kit
Jewelry assembly kit

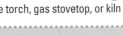

Firing Schedule LOW-FIRE
Butane torch, gas stovetop, or kiln

1 Roll the clay to 1.5 mm/6 cards thick [A].

2 If you're using a texture mat, roll over the sheet to texture the clay [B]. If you're using a ball to apply texture, place the clay on the ball and roll the clay gently but with firm pressure. Don't make the clay too thin.

3 Cut out a circle using a craft knife or cutter [C].

4 Using a coffee stirrer or small straw, punch a hole at the top of the pendant [D].

If you're **making** a basketball or football pendant, use the ball itself to create texture.

If you'd like **realistic details** on your pendant, add those before you personalize it. For a football, draw laces. For a basketball or baseball, create the lines of the ball. If you're making a jersey, scribe the seams of the shirt.

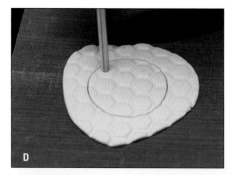

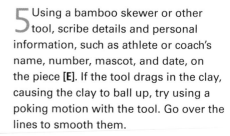

5 Using a bamboo skewer or other tool, scribe details and personal information, such as athlete or coach's name, number, mascot, and date, on the piece [E]. If the tool drags in the clay, causing the clay to ball up, try using a poking motion with the tool. Go over the lines to smooth them.

6 Dry the piece completely.

7 Use mini files or sanding sticks to smooth the edges, sanding on an angle to create a beveled edge [F].

We molded these pendants from buttons.

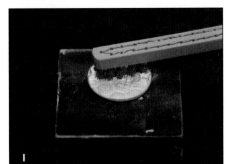

8 Smooth the front and back with 600-grit sandpaper, sanding pads, or polishing papers **[G]**, taking care to avoid any texture. If you are creating a piece with a smooth finish, progress through higher sanding grits to make the front of the piece as smooth as possible before firing. Smooth the back of the piece with a higher grit.

9 Using a dry paintbrush, brush any dust from the inside of the letters. Fire the piece following the low-fire schedule (we torch-fired our pendant) **[H]**. The pendant may be quenched to cool, because it is a solid silver piece.

10 Brush the piece with a stainless steel or brass brush **[I]**.

11 Tumble the piece for an hour or so or burnish with an agate burnisher **[J]**.

12 Use liver of sulfur to add a dark patina. Apply jewelry polish with a polishing cloth to shine the front and bring out the contrast of the lettering **[K]**.

13 Attach a jump ring to the hanging hole.

A gift for Coach

Do you know a coach who deserves an extra-special gift? A pendant with the coach's name and year can be attached to the lanyard that holds her whistle. Or help each team player to create an original charm that represents herself or himself. Attach with jump rings to a chain, add a clasp, and you'll have a one-of-a-kind coach's bracelet.

Keys, Please!
key chain

A key chain is one of hundreds of ways we accessorize ourselves and our property, and it offers nearly limitless opportunities for customization.

This project shows how to make a pure silver accessory that is trendy, personalized, and precious. Choose a mini version of the auto driven by the owner. Or how about one that he or she aspires to own?

quick reference

MATERIALS & TOOLS
40 grams low-fire silver clay
Paste clay
Detailed toy car (no larger than 3 in./76 mm)
Two-part molding compound
2–3 large fine-silver screw eyes
Key ring

TOOL KITS
Wet-clay tool kit
Greenware tool kit
Finishing tool kit
Jewelry assembly tools

Firing Schedule LOW-FIRE
Kiln only; because this piece is larger than 25 grams, it can't be fired with a torch or on a stovetop

1 Clean the toy car gently with warm water and mild soap to remove oils or dirt in the surface detail of the car. Dry completely.

2 Knead together equal amounts of the two-part molding compound until the color is solid (each part should be about the size of the car). Form the compound into a tube just a bit longer than the car. Press the car firmly and evenly into the compound, just deep enough to capture the detail of one side of the car. Leave the car in place while the mold sets **[A]**.

3 Remove the toy car **[B]**. Condition the mold, using a stiff paintbrush to reach all the nooks and crannies.

4 Open all the silver clay, kneading it together if you have multiple packages. Press the clay firmly into the mold, filling the entire bottom area **[C]**.

5 Allow the clay to set for about 5 minutes. Gently turn the mold upside down on the nonstick surface and carefully peel the mold away from the clay **[D]**. Handle the mold and the metal clay gingerly to prevent the design from becoming warped.

6 Use a craft knife to trim excess clay from the molded clay **[E]**. Remove any excess from the back of the molded clay.

7 Insert 2 or 3 screw eyes into the thickest edge of the silver **[F]**. Embed the findings deeply, capturing the base of the round eye in the clay. Add a little bit of paste at the base of the eyes for additional strength.

Plan the spacing between the screw eyes so you'll be able to attach the key ring.

A

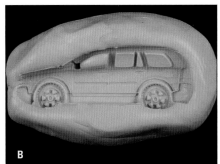
B

C

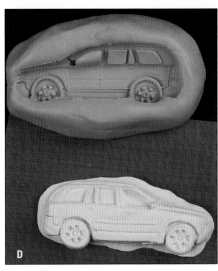
D

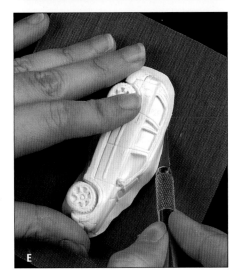
E

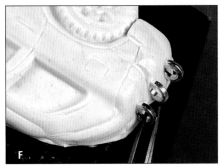
F

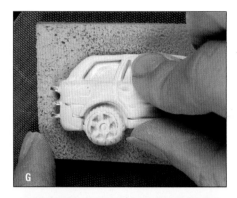

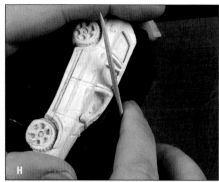

8 Dry the piece completely. Because the car is large and thick, it's a good idea to let the piece to dry overnight in a dehydrator or for several days if air drying.

9 Place the piece design side up on a sanding pad or coarse sandpaper (approximately 220 grit). Sand the back flat, supporting the whole piece from the top and sides with your fingers [G]. Repeat the sanding process with higher grits up to 1200 grit until you see a nice, smooth sheen.

10 Use mini files or sanding sticks to smooth any sharp edges [H]. Smooth the surface of the vehicle with 600–1200 grit sandpaper or sanding pads, being careful not to erase any fine details of the car.

11 Fire the piece in a kiln following the low-fire schedule. Allow the piece to come to room temperature. Brush, burnish, and use a liver of sulfur solution to accentuate the car's details [I]. Polish with jewelry polish and cloth.

12 Attach the key ring to the screw eyes [J].

Don't take chances with this much clay.
Make sure it's completely dry prior to firing or the moisture within the piece will turn to steam and, in escaping, damage your piece.

Anything—including a monkey climbing a photo frame—is fair game for molding.

See Spot Sparkle
pet tag

A pet owner will often tell you that life would be incomplete without animals. Our pets comfort us, attend to us, and ask for nothing in return but a treat and a belly rub. Once you've been touched by a furry family member, life—and your home—is never the same.

This project recognizes the importance our pets have. They deserve to be treated to the same beautiful adornment that we like for ourselves.

quick reference

MATERIALS & TOOLS
10 grams low-fire silver clay
Syringe clay with medium tip
Pet-themed silicone mold (dog bone, cat silhouette, paw print, etc.)
Pin vise with 1.5 mm bit
Jump ring

TOOL KITS
Wet-clay tool kit
Greenware tool kit
Finishing tool kit
Jewelry assembly kit

Firing Schedule LOW-FIRE
Butane torch, gas stovetop, or kiln

1 Condition the silicone mold and press the clay into the mold, working it from the middle toward the ends. Press repeatedly to remove all air bubbles and minimize any folds in the clay **[A]**. Press the clay as flat as possible on the back, pinching off and storing any extra clay.

2 When the clay is dry to the touch, remove it from the mold by inverting the silicone and gently flexing it to pop the clay shape out. Be careful not to distort the clay by over-flexing it.

3 Place the silver shape faceup on a nonstick sheet. Use the craft knife to trim the excess clay from the edges of the tag **[B]**. Dry the piece to bone dry.

4 Smooth the back of the shape by moving it back and forth on a sanding surface, holding it gently in several spots to distribute the force of your fingers **[C]**. Sand the back until it is smooth. Gently smooth the front of the piece, eliminating lines or divots.

5 Use the paintbrush to moisten the front of the tag. This will help the syringe clay detail adhere better to the base shape.

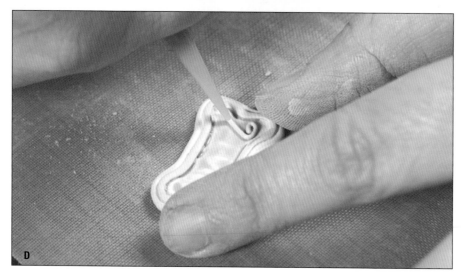

6 Lightly write the pet's name on the tag with pencil, and use syringe clay to trace over the lines **[D]**. Take your time! Nudge any errant syringe lines into place with the moist paintbrush. Use the brush to gently tap the syringe down and increase its bond with the tag **[E]**. Dry the piece completely.

> **You can make the shape** by using small cutters designed for pet treats, too. Roll the clay to 2 mm thick.

7 Feel the piece for rough or sharp areas. Buff these segments very gently with sanding material until the sharpness is gone.

8 Use the pin vise to drill a small hole in the top center of the tag [F]. Only very gentle pressure is necessary.

9 Fire the piece according to the low-fire schedule.

10 When cool, brush with a stainless steel or brass brush, giving the piece a matte finish [G].

11 Burnish the piece with an agate burnisher, giving all the raised areas a high shine [H], or tumble for 1–2 hours.

12 Use liver of sulfur solution to add a dark patina. Apply jewelry polish with a polishing cloth. The patina will come off the surfaces you reach with the polishing cloth, leaving contrast around the pet's name. Add the jump ring to the tag, and attach to your furry friend's collar.

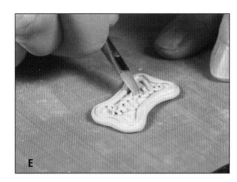

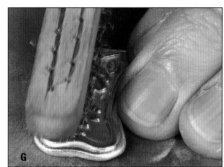
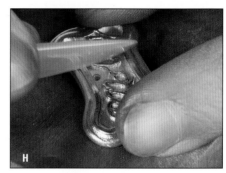

Syringe wrangling

The easiest way we've found for holding the syringe is to rest it in the palm of your dominant hand with your fingers wrapped around the barrel and your thumb on the depressor. Use wrist movement to guide the line of clay being placed. This will help you get the best control of the tip and is the least tiring. Holding the syringe as though you were giving an injection puts all of the stress in your first two fingertips and thumb, making it hard to control where the clay line falls.

Try not to drag the syringe on the surface. Touch down to anchor the start of the clay line and lift the tip as you extrude. Place the line where you want it and gently touch down to anchor the end for best results.

Best Friends Forever
lock-and-key pendants

Our friends share our lives, offering support, consolation, laughter, and joy. This lock-and-key set is a tiny reminder of love between best friends. Give both pieces to a friend, divide the set between the two of you, or make two sets. You'll never forget where the key resides.

quick reference

MATERIALS & TOOLS
14 grams low-fire silver clay for each set
Syringe clay with fine tip
1-in. (26 mm) oval cutter
½-in. (13 mm) oval cutter
Rubber sheet for carving (or pencil eraser)
Small key mold
Large jump ring
Fine-silver screw eye

TOOL KITS
Wet-clay tool kit
Greenware tool kit
Finishing tool kit
Jewelry assembly kit

Firing Schedule LOW-FIRE
Butane torch, gas stovetop, or kiln

1 Draw a keyhole shape that is about ⁵⁄₁₆-in. (8 mm) tall onto the rubber carving sheet or pencil eraser. Carve away the surrounding sheet or eraser, leaving a deep stamp **[A]**.

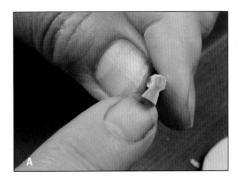

2 Roll 10 grams of clay to 2 mm/8 cards thick **[B]**.

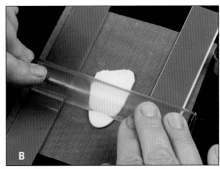

3 Use the larger oval cutter to cut an oval **[C]**. Store excess clay.

4 Turn the smaller cutter sideways and cut another oval from the top of the larger oval to make the bar section of the lock **[D]**.

5 Stamp the keyhole in the center of the lock shape **[E]**. Don't go all the way through the clay.

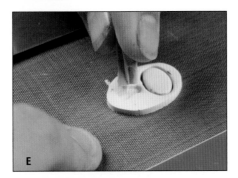

6 With a needle tool, scribe a short, horizontal line on each side of the lock at the point where the curved bar meets the body of the lock **[F]**.

7 Add a small dot of syringe clay to each side of the lock, under the scribed lines **[G]**. Smooth the dots with a moist paintbrush, flattening them and attaching them securely.

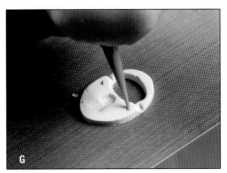

8 Use the needle tool to scribe a line through the dots, giving them the appearance of the top of a screw **[H]**.

9 Let the lock shape dry completely.

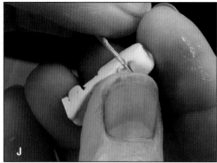

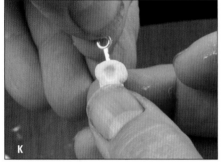

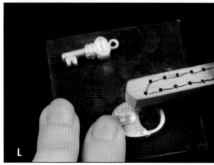

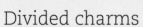

I

J

K

L

M

We used a purchased key mold, but it's easy to mold your own from a key charm. We carved the keyhole stamp from a pencil eraser.

10 Lightly condition the key mold. Using firm pressure, press leftover clay into the mold. Smooth the back with your thumb, removing excess clay and flattening the back of the key shape **[I]**.

11 When the clay is dry to the touch, gently bend the mold to remove the key. Trim excess clay using a craft knife. Use a needle tool to scribe detail into the front of the key **[J]**.

12 Insert a fine-silver screw eye into the rounded top of the key **[K]**. Add a little syringe clay to help secure the screw eye, smoothing the clay with a moist paintbrush. Let the key dry completely. Use syringe clay to add lines on the back of the key to duplicate the detail on the front. Dry completely.

13 Use mini files, sanding pads, or polishing papers to smooth all surfaces of the lock and key. Fire following the low-fire schedule.

14 Brush the pieces with a brass or stainless steel brush **[L]**. For a shinier finish, use an agate burnisher or tumbler.

15 Attach a jump ring to the bar of the lock and the screw eye of the key, and string on a chain or cord **[M]**.

Get personal
Scribe names or initials on each piece before it's completely dry. The friends can trade keys. For more than two friends, make one lock for each person and enough keys so that each friend has a key from every other pal.

Divided charms
Make a divided charm for a pair of best friends, like a broken heart or positive and negative shapes. Or they may enjoy other related pairs, such as a sun and moon, symmetric flowers, or yin and yang symbols.

Quotable
impressed link bracelet

This bracelet is designed for a high school or college graduate to recognize achievement while offering guiding words for the future. It's easy to modify and makes a great gift for other life events as well.

This project uses stamps that you create. Use the pattern on the next page for reference, set up the quote in a favorite font, and then follow the instructions for creating photopolymer plates on p. 104. The smaller links hold the name of the recipient, the school, and graduation year. If you'd rather not make your own stamps, you can use a purchased stamp for the quote, a mini typesetting stamp, or scribe your messages in the clay.

quick reference

MATERIALS & TOOLS
40 grams low-fire silver clay
Photopolymer plate for each link
Bracelet mandrel or soup can
Toggle clasp
Jump rings (approximately 25, depending on wrist size)
Graph mat or gridded paper (optional)
Fine-tip permanent marker (optional)

TOOL KITS
Wet-clay tool kit
Greenware tool kit
Finishing tool kit
Jewelry assembly kit

Firing Schedule LOW-FIRE
Kiln only; the center link is too large to be fired with a torch or on a stovetop

Before you begin: Make photopolymer plates

This bracelet has three links (see pattern for various sizes). Make the center link no larger than 1½ x 2¼ in. (38 x 57 mm). Allow space for the holes as you set up the text for the stamp. Create three stamps, one for each link, following the instructions for making photopolymer plates on p. 104. Condition the stamps before use.

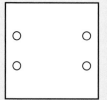

Here are a few additional tips for this project:
- **Use a clear, easy-to-read font. Make the lettering white and the background solid black.**
- **Print two copies of the images onto transparency film and layer them so that the black background is especially dark.**
- **An option is to write the words by hand. Use a photocopier to reduce the handwriting and copy it onto the transparency film.**

1 Place the graph mat on your work surface, and place a nonstick sheet over the graph mat. The graph mat will help as you roll and trim rectangles.

Graph mat, available from metal clay suppliers, is ruled with lines that are ¼ in. (6.5 mm) apart. You could substitute a sheet of graph paper or draw your own ruled guide on transparency film.

2 Open all packages of clay, saving one empty package, and massage the clay together. Roll the clay 2 mm/ 8 cards thick into a rectangle slightly larger than the dimensions of the large link **[A]**. (It may help to draw the targeted dimensions on the nonstick sheet with permanent marker before you roll.)

3 With the craft knife, trim the clay to the size of the largest link **[B]**.

4 Remove the extra clay, place it on the second nonstick sheet, and cover it loosely with a damp paper towel to keep it moist. (Or you can return the clay to the reclosable packaging, remove air, and seal tightly.)

5 Center the conditioned quote stamp over the rolled clay. With gentle but firm pressure, push the stamp evenly into the clay **[C]**. Remove the stamp by gently flexing the photopolymer and allowing the clay to fall away from the stamp. Set the stamped piece aside, and cover it loosely with damp paper towel.

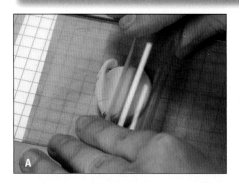

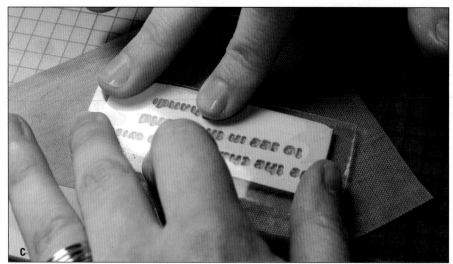

6 Roll clay to fit the two smaller links, trim, and stamp the links. Cover the small links with damp paper towel until you are ready to work with them again, and store any unused clay.

7 Use a narrow straw to punch two holes on each connecting edge of each link (see pattern) **[D]**. It may help to position the links in order as they will be linked in the bracelet.

8 Keeping the clay on the nonstick sheet, drape the large link over the bracelet mandrel or soup can so it dries with a curved shape **[E]**. The smaller links can remain flat while drying. Let all pieces dry completely.

9 Smooth the edges with a mini file or sanding stick **[F]**. Gently round the corners and bevel the edges. It takes only very soft pressure to smooth the corners and edges. Use the rubber block to help support the pieces as you sand. Be careful not to apply too much pressure, especially to the large, curved link; the clay is brittle at this stage.

10 Use 600-grit sandpaper or a sanding pad to smooth the edges and the surfaces of the links **[G]**. Progress to higher grits, up to at least 1200, to create a smooth finish. Use a round mini file to smooth the holes.

Dry the links
on small pieces
of nonstick sheet,
each about 4 in.
(10 cm) square.

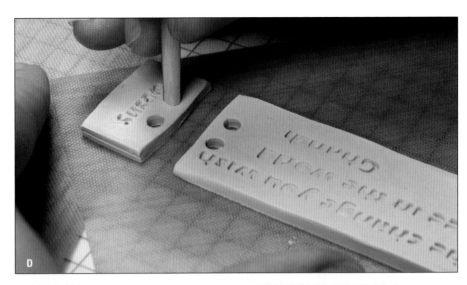

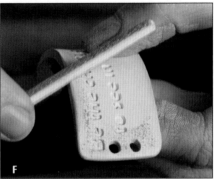

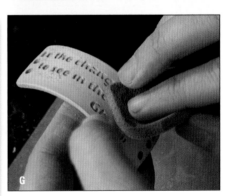

A broken link

If the large link breaks as you're smoothing it, no worries—the finished bracelet will still turn out great. Keep refining the outside edges of the link pieces, avoiding the broken edges. When all pre-fire smoothing is done, apply a line of syringe clay along the cracked edge, and push the pieces together. Place the link on its side. Use a moist paintbrush to smooth the seam. Allow to dry completely, then buff the seam lightly with 1200-grit sandpaper or a fine sanding pad until the seam is no longer noticeable. If you still see some gaps, you can apply more syringe clay, dry, and sand again.

Sizing a link bracelet

This bracelet fits a small wrist, about 5½ in. (14 cm) in circumference. To make a longer bracelet, add extra jump rings between the links.

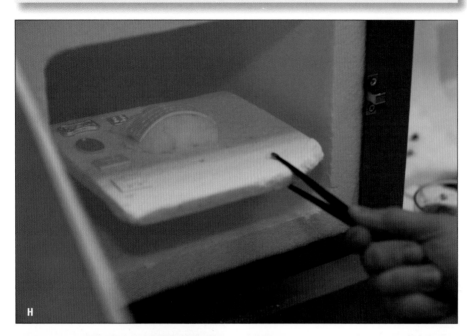

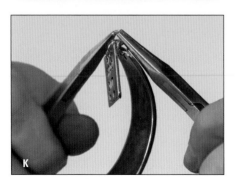

11 Fire the large link on fiber board with the quote facing up and fiber blanket packed under the curve for support **[H]**. Place the smaller links directly on the fiber board. Fire according to the low-fire schedule. Let the pieces cool to room temperature.

12 Brush the links with the stainless steel or brass brush **[I]**. If you like this matte finish, polish with a drop of metal polish on a cloth; no further finishing is necessary. (We don't recommend patina on a matte piece because it settles in the scratches and looks messy.) If you'd like a mirror finish, tumble-polish or use an agate burnisher or wet/dry sandpapers. If desired, add patina with liver of sulfur, then polish the piece to bring out the highlights **[J]**, leaving dark patina in the lettering.

13 To assemble the bracelet: Close four jump rings and open about 20. Pick up an open jump ring, string it through an end hole in the large link, pick up a closed jump ring, and close the open ring. Repeat on all the remaining holes of the large link.

Pick up an open ring and attach a closed ring and the hole of a small link. Close the ring **[K]**. Repeat with the remaining hole on the same edge of the small link; repeat on the other end of the large link with the other small link.

On one end of the bracelet, attach a jump ring to each hole on the small link and close the jump rings. Repeat on the other end.

Open a jump ring, connect two end rings and the round clasp half, and close the ring.

On the other end, open a jump ring, connect the two end rings, and close the jump ring. Add 3–5 jump rings to create a short tail, connecting the toggle end of the clasp to the last jump ring. The tail gives the clasp flexibility and makes it easier to close.

Personalize the bracelet even more by making the toggle from silver clay (see p. 103).

Wealthy & Healthy
baby spoon

The gift of a silver spoon to a newborn child is a wish that the child's life be bountiful and that wealth will travel with them as they grow, just like the easily portable spoon. But there's also a hygienic side to this gift: Pure silver is a powerful antibacterial agent. Feeding a child with a silver utensil is a way to begin life with good health as well.

In this project, you'll mold three components from lump clay—the bear, the stem, and the spoon bowl—and join them using paste clay to make a spoon.

quick reference

MATERIALS & TOOLS
17 grams low-fire silver clay
Paste clay
Two-part molding compound
Teddy bear button
Heart border mold
Oval bowl mold, spoon, or
   small light bulb

TOOL KITS
Wet-clay tool kit
Greenware tool kit
Finishing tool kit

Firing Schedule LOW-FIRE
Kiln only; the stem is too long to be fired with a torch or on a stovetop

1 Blend marble-sized parts of the two-part molding compound until the colors are completely blended. Press the bear button facedown into the compound until the back is level with the sides of the mold. When the mold is firm, remove the button **[A]**.

2 Condition the mold. Press about 7 grams of clay into the mold, filling the entire area. Allow the clay to set for about 5 minutes. Turn the mold over, holding it above the nonstick surface, and carefully remove the silver clay. Handle the mold and the metal clay

gently to avoid distorting the molded bear. (If the clay bear warps or twists, knead it and quickly press it into the mold a second time.) Use a craft knife to trim excess clay from the edges of the molded bear **[B]**. Set the bear aside to dry completely.

3 To mold the stem, condition the border mold. Roll about 8 grams of clay into a snake at least 6 in. (15 cm) long. Press or roll the clay firmly into the mold, filling at least eight of the hearts **[C]**. (We filled 14 hearts and used the extras to make a matching pair of earrings for mom.)

4 Allow the clay to set for a moment, then trim the back flat with a tissue blade **[D]**.

5 Remove the strip of clay from the mold **[E]**, and place it on a small piece of nonstick surface. Nudge the strip into a straight line with the edge of the border mold. Dry the piece completely.

6 Roll the remaining clay to a thickness of 1.5 mm/6 cards) **[F]**.

7 Shape the clay around the oval bowl mold, and trim the edges to fit **[G]**. (Use an actual spoon bowl or a small light bulb as a form if you don't have a bowl mold.) Allow all pieces to dry completely.

8 Sand the back of the bear smooth, starting with 600 grit and working up to 2000 grit **[H]**. Smooth the back of the stem and the inner and outer surfaces of the spoon bowl in the same way.

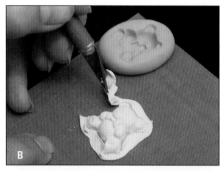

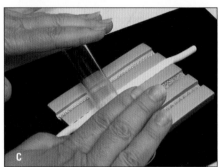

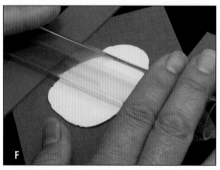

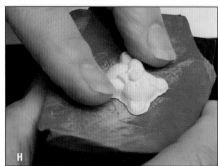

Matching earrings for Mom!

9 Using a mini file, smooth the edges of the bear, removing all rough spots and excess clay **[I]**.

10 Use a mini file to smooth the edges of the stem **[J]**. Using a craft knife or tissue blade, trim the stem to the desired length.

11 With a moist paintbrush, apply a bit of paste clay to the bowl at the point where the stem will attach **[K]**. Attach the stem to the bowl at a slight angle. Prop the pieces in position while the paste dries completely. Turn the piece over and reinforce the join with additional paste on the back **[L]**. Let dry completely.

12 Add more paste if necessary to secure the join. Let dry completely between applications. Sand the join until smooth.

13 Repeat the pasting and smoothing process to attach the bear at the top of the stem **[M]**.

14 Kiln-fire the piece following the low-fire schedule. Support the spoon, propping the angled bowl with pieces of fiber blanket **[N]**. Allow the spoon to cool to room temperature (you may quench it in water for quicker cooling).

15 For a matte finish, brush the spoon with a stainless steel or brass brush **[O]**.

16 For a high shine, tumble-polish the spoon for two hours **[P]**. If you don't have a tumbler, burnish the spoon with an agate burnisher. Finish shining with metal polish and a polishing cloth.

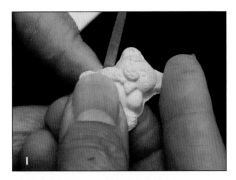

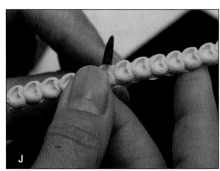

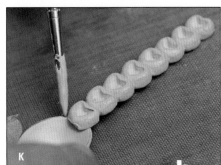

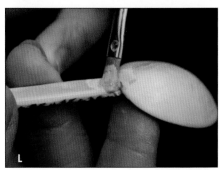

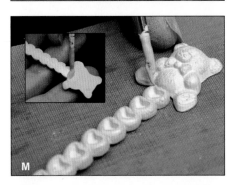

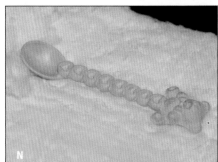

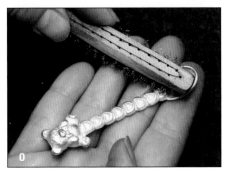

Celtic Charm
pendant

The Celtic knot is an elegant design, flowing and soft. Traditionally, different knots represent different concepts and can be incredibly complex. Each knot seems to have no beginning and no end, winding on forever.

While this project is introduced as a Celtic knot, it can be modified countless ways to accommodate the taste of your giftee. Some knot shapes work better than others for using syringe clay. Look for knots with clear lines to follow, several places where the syringe lines can cross for support, and open spaces no larger than ½ in. (13 mm) across. See p. 100 for some patterns, or create your own.

quick reference

MATERIALS
Low-fire syringe clay with large tip
Paste clay
Knot pattern to size
Clear tape
2 jump rings

TOOL KITS
Wet-clay tool kit
Greenware tool kit
Finishing tool kit
Jewelry assembly kit

OPTIONAL
CZs
Tweezers
Isopropyl alcohol
Cotton swab

Firing Schedule LOW-FIRE
Butane torch, gas stovetop, or kiln

1 Center the nonstick work surface over the pattern so that you can see the pattern lines. Tape the surface to the pattern.

2 Trace the pattern, holding the syringe at a 45-degree angle a few millimeters above the work surface. Drop the clay into place; don't touch the nozzle on the work surface as you put down a line or you will squish it. Let the syringe clay cross over itself, joining where the lines intersect. Try to center the lines of clay over the template lines for the best possible symmetry. This first pass will form the base of three layers **[A]**.

3 Use a moist paintbrush to reposition any lines that have strayed from the pattern lines. Use the brush to tap down any areas where the lines cross, solidifying the joins **[B]**.

4 Let the piece dry completely, leaving it in place on the nonstick sheet.

5 Using the first layer of syringe clay as a guide, apply another layer of syringe clay directly over the first **[C]**. Repeat step 3. If you'd like to add CZs, add them now (see p. 102). Use the tweezers to embed the CZs in areas of the design where the syringe clay is wide enough to hold them. They will be captured when you add a third layer of syringe clay. Let the piece dry completely.

6 Add a final layer of syringe clay to the piece, following the lines of the dry shape, and use a moist brush to reposition the syringe clay as needed. Remoisten the brush, and pat down and smooth all joins **[D]**. Let the syringe clay shape set for one minute at room temperature. Very gently, use a moist brush to smooth the syringe clay, shaping it to appear more fluid. If you added CZs, be sure they are trapped between the second and third layers

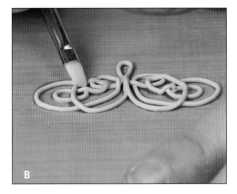

of syringe clay. Use the paintbrush to shape the syringe clay over the CZs, covering only the girdle and leaving the table visible (see p. 102). Dry completely.

Make a pair of smaller knots into dainty earrings.

E

F

G

7 Use the brush to add a thick layer of paste around the edges of the syringe clay to seal the layers. Cover the perimeter of the whole piece with a smooth coating of paste [E]. Dry completely.

8 Place the piece on a rubber block. Use a flexible sanding pad to gently buff the piece, removing any sharp areas on the surface. Sand the sides as well. Sand very gently; the loops of the knot are extremely fragile [F]. If you added CZs, use denatured alcohol on a cotton swab to remove any silver clay dust from the stones' surface.

9 Fire the piece according to the low-fire schedule. Allow the piece to cool to room temperature. If it doesn't have CZs, you can quench it in water.

10 Place the piece on a rubber block and brush the piece with a stainless steel or brass brush [G].

11 Burnish all angles with an agate burnisher for a high shine. Be careful not to accidentally pry the syringe lines away from each other with the burnisher, causing a crack. For greater shine and a smoother surface, tumble the piece for two hours and polish.

12 Depending on the shape of the knot and your preference, attach one or two jump rings so that the piece hangs well. Add a smooth chain that accentuates the smooth Celtic knot design or, if you've added gemstones, use cord or ribbon to coordinate with the color of the stones.

To attach a syringe tip, remove the end cap and push the tip firmly while screwing it onto the tube. To dispense the clay, hold the syringe in your fist, grasping it with your fingers and depressing the plunger with your thumb.

Does your knot have a good spot for some sparkle? Place CZs before you add the final layer of syringe clay.

3 Silver Plus

Birthstones
link bracelet

This bracelet links family or friends together no matter how far apart they may be physically. Each link states the person's name and includes a CZ birthstone for a splash of color.

For a variation, consider a theme that's meaningful for the recipient. Someone active in a place of worship might appreciate the terms *Faith, Spirit, Hope, Worship, Love* on the links. A young athlete might prefer *Focus, Speed, Strength, Effort, Victory* with gemstones in the colors of favorite sports teams. Another variation is a bracelet for someone facing cancer or a cancer survivor, with the terms *Courage, Hope, Strength, Life, Cure*. The gemstones add vibrancy to the piece but aren't essential.

quick reference

MATERIALS & TOOLS
21 grams low-fire silver clay
Syringe clay with medium tip
Small clay cutter for link shape
5 mm CZs (1 for each link)
Isopropyl alcohol
Cotton swab
Jump rings (about 12)
Toggle clasp

TOOL KITS
Wet-clay tool kit
Greenware tool kit
Finishing tool kit
Jewelry assembly kit

Firing Schedule LOW-FIRE
Butane torch, gas stovetop, or kiln

The birthstone chart on p. 101 can help as you choose CZ colors.

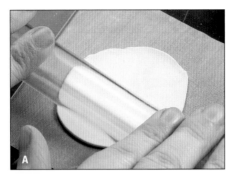

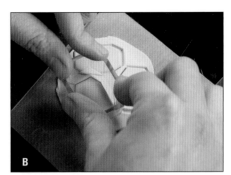

1 Roll the clay 2 mm/8 cards thick [A]. If you have multiple packages of clay, open only one at a time as needed.

2 Use the cutter to cut several link shapes at a time [B]. Work quickly, assembly-line style, for best results. Repackage the clay scraps.

3 While each link shape is still moist, scribe a name or word using a gentle poking motion like tattooing [C], allowing room at each end for jump ring holes. Go back with the scribing tool and smooth out the insides of the letters. Use a coffee stirrer to punch a hole where a CZ will be placed later. Store any excess clay, including the bits from inside the straw. Set aside to dry.

4 Repeat steps 2–3 until you have as many links as you need.

5 Using a pin vise, drill holes for the jump rings at least 2 mm from the edges of the clay [D].

6 Dry the links completely. To prevent warping, flip the links over several times as they dry. (Letting the links air dry at least overnight is the best option, if you have time.) The links must be bone dry.

7 Smooth the edges of the links with sanding sticks, an emery board, or mini files [E].

8 Use a round-tipped file to smooth and deepen the scribed letters [F] and to smooth the insides of the holes.

9 Sand the front, back, and edges with polishing papers or sanding pads [G]

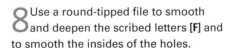

Do a little math
Consider shrinkage and the recipient's wrist measurement as you plan the size and number of links. Our finished links are 1 in. (26 mm) long, and we linked five of them to create a bracelet for a small wrist.

SILVER PLUS

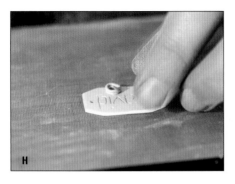

10 Use syringe clay to make the CZ setting: Outline the hole made for the CZ with three layers of syringe-clay rings, one on top of the other [**H**]. Use tweezers to center the CZ in the moist setting [**I**]. Gently press the CZ until the setting surrounds the edges of the stone, even with the flat top of the CZ. Use a moist paintbrush to smooth the setting into place [**J**]. Allow the clay to dry completely.

11 Gently buff the setting and surrounding areas with polishing pads or paper until smooth.

12 Clean the surfaces of the stone carefully with isopropyl alcohol on a cotton swab to remove any silver dust.

13 Repeat steps 10–12 for each CZ setting.

14 Fire the pieces according to the low-fire schedule. Let the links cool slowly to room temperature.

15 For the colorful matte patina as shown on p. 56, do not brush or burnish the links before dipping them into liver of sulfur solution. Clean the silver with a paste made of baking soda and water, then dip the still-white pieces into the solution. Rinse as soon as you see color you like.

16 Link the bracelet together with jump rings, and use jump rings to attach a clasp half at each end.

For more information on setting gemstones, see p. 102.

Create a custom clasp
To step up the personalization of this project, make a custom toggle closure. Learn how on p. 103.

We created some square links and a custom clasp from silver clay for this version.

From "Sorry!" to Silver
pendant

Nearly every family has one—the cherished china heirloom that passes from household to household through the generations. Sometimes it sits as a sentimental centerpiece for family gatherings, sometimes it holds the traditional favorite dessert, sometimes it hangs proudly on prominent wall space. But accidents happen. What do you do when a treasured artifact is broken?

You set it in pure silver, of course! Any china, stoneware, or ceramic item can be successfully fired with low-fire silver clay, provided the kiln is set to heat and cool gradually. In this way, we turn beloved shards into beautiful, silver-clad art that many friends or family members will enjoy.

quick reference

MATERIALS & TOOLS
5–7 grams low-fire silver clay
ACS Overlay Paste
Low-fire syringe clay with medium or
   fine tip
Broken piece of china, stoneware,
   or ceramic plate
Isopropyl alcohol
Cotton swab
Empty syringe for extruding (optional)

TOOL KITS
Wet-clay tool kit
Greenware tool kit
Finishing tool kit
Jewelry assembly kit

Firing Schedule
CERAMICS WITH OVERLAY
Kiln only; slow ramp. See
details on p. 101.

1 Clean the shard with isopropyl alcohol on a cotton swab. The piece must be free of dust or oil for best results.

2 Paint full-strength Overlay Paste on the edges of the broken shard [A], Make the layer thick enough to cover any sharp edges. Paint a little paste on the front and back edges of the piece to give the piece the look of a bezel setting.

3 Dry completely. Overlay Paste dries more quickly than lump clay, but be sure that the paste is truly dry.

4 Use polishing pads or papers to sand the edges of the Overlay Paste [B]. If the paste seems thin, possibly exposing any part of the shard edge during firing, add another layer of paste, dry completely, and smooth again. Return the fine powder that's removed to the jar.

5 Add decorative detail to the edges with syringe clay [C]. Avoid the edge where you plan to attach the bail. Use syringe clay to extend a design that appears on the shard or to create a new pattern. The medium syringe tip will work well for this, or use a fine tip to add delightfully light and delicate lines. Dry the clay completely.

6 Using polishing papers or sanding pads, gently buff any rough edges from the decoration [D]. The syringe clay is extremely delicate before firing.

7 To create a fancy, coiled bail, load a small bit of low-fire clay in an empty syringe [E] and extrude it to form a snake [F] about 8 in. (20 cm) long. If you don't have an empty syringe, roll low-fire clay to form a thin snake. Wrap the snake around a short length of bamboo skewer, and attach the resulting coil to the top of the piece with Overlay Paste. Attach the coil ends to the back of the piece for extra support [G]. Paint a little Overlay Paste on the coil where it meets the shard.

8 Let the bail dry completely. Don't worry about the skewer in the bail; it will fire in place and burn away in the kiln.

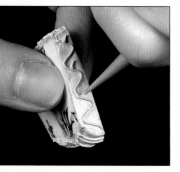

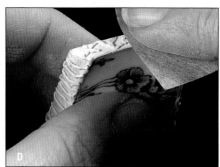

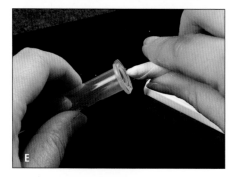

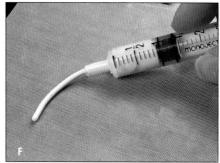

Don't be tempted to make the bail from syringe clay! Roll or extrude lump clay to make a sturdy bail. See p. 9 for tips on preparing an empty syringe for extruding.

9 Add a little more Overlay Paste around the edges of the bail in any area that looks thin. This attachment must be very strong. Dry the piece thoroughly.

10 Smooth the attachments where the bail meets the shard with polishing papers or sanding pads. Gently smooth the bail as much as possible [H]. Use a toothpick to scratch away any large areas of dried paste that peek out from underneath the ends of the coil on the back [I].

11 Clean the surface of the stoneware again with alcohol.

12 Using the Overlay Paste cap as a cup, dilute a few drops of paste with a few drops of water. Using a fine paintbrush, accent the design on the shard with the diluted Overlay Paste [J]. A mini liner paintbrush will work well to add intricate lines or reach small, textured areas. Allow the paste to dry completely. Return any diluted paste to the jar.

13 Clean the shard again. Use a toothpick or bamboo skewer to scratch away any excess dried paste. Clean the areas around the silver embellishments with alcohol.

14 Fire the piece in a programmable kiln. Follow the Ceramics With Overlay schedule, heating and cooling no more than 500°F (260°C) per hour to avoid thermal shock in the shard. Hold at 1200°F (650°C) for 30 minutes, and allow the kiln to cool very slowly. For your safety, never open a kiln with a ceramic object inside until it has come to room temperature.

15 Brush the edges of the piece with a brass or stainless steel brush for a matte finish [K].

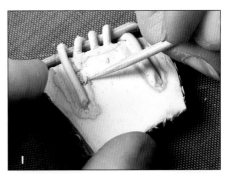

16 For a greater shine, use an agate burnisher on all the raised syringe areas [L] and on the bail.

Tumbling is usually not a good option for a piece that has only Overlay Paste on the surface, but if the paste is covered with syringe clay as it is here, the silver should hold up if tumble-polished for no more than 30 minutes.

Two small shards make great earrings. Bend the shanks of two fine silver screw eyes and embed them in thick layers of Overlay Paste.

You'll fire with a slow ramp because ceramic and stoneware items can handle high temperatures but need to adjust slowly. Changing the temperature too quickly can cause thermal shock, cracking the ceramic.

Not So Tacky
tie tack

The fantastic thing about a tie tack is that it can be as outrageous or as simple as the gentleman who wears it prefers. We've seen tie tacks that are small, large, shiny, matte, whimsical, geometric, even ones that blink or have sound effects. Some guys are just way out there with their style, while others are more reserved and would rather have their tie tack blend in with their outfit.

We'll show you how to make a simple, elegant, and geometric design with just a bit of bling. Because it's fairly easy to modify this project, we threw in a few variations here.

quick reference

MATERIALS & TOOLS
10 grams low-fire silver clay
Tie tack base, at least 5 mm
3 mm CZ
Isopropyl alcohol
Cotton swab
Jeweler's epoxy
Round cutter (optional)

TOOL KITS
Wet-clay tool kit
Greenware tool kit
Finishing tool kit

Firing Schedule LOW-FIRE
Butane torch, gas stovetop, or kiln

1 Roll the clay to 2 mm/8 cards thick [A].

2 Use either the craft knife or a cutter to cut a disc out of the clay [B]. Repackage the scraps.

3 Use a coffee stirrer to make a hole in the clay at least 2 mm away from one edge. With tweezers, place the CZ and press until the flat top (called the *table*) is even with the surface of the clay [C]. Let dry completely.

> **The CZ** is set using a technique called a clay capture for a very clean look (see p. 102).

4 Remove any sharp edges from the disc with the mini files, using the rubber block for support [D]. With a succession of finer-grit polishing papers or sanding pads, smooth the disc to prepare it for a mirror finish [E].

5 Using an edge of a triangular mini file, carve long, straight lines into the face of the disc, forming a geometric pattern [F]. (See the photo of our finished piece for guidance or create your own pattern.) Smooth the surface to remove any divots or dust, and brush dust from inside the engraved lines.

6 Fire the clay according to the low-fire schedule. Do not quench this piece; allow the clay to return to room temperature slowly to protect the CZ.

7 Brush with a stainless steel or brass brush [G]. For a shiny finish, tumble-polish for two hours or burnish with an agate burnisher.

8 Brush with a baking soda paste, then use liver of sulfur to add patina.

9 Polish the front of the tie tack with jewelry polish and a soft cloth to remove some patina on the surface, leaving the lines dark for contrast. Avoid getting polish on the back of the tie tack.

10 Clean the back with alcohol to remove all oils or residue. Attach the base of the tie tack finding to the back of the silver tie tack with jeweler's epoxy [H, I]. Let the epoxy dry for 24 hours.

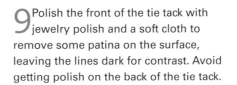

SILVER PLUS

Captured Moments
silver and resin pendant

Many mementos can't be exposed to the high temperatures that silver needs to sinter. In this project, you create a fired silver frame and then suspend your special item in resin within it. If you don't have an extruder, you can create the frame simply by rolling and trimming the clay.

What you choose to embed in the resin is entirely up to you: buttons from outgrown outfits, snaps, baby jewelry, snips of lace or trim from too-small clothing, or even organic items such as locks of hair, dried flowers, or small shells. Add embellishments like little pearls, beads, or ribbon, or sparklies like sequins and glitter.

quick reference

MATERIALS & TOOLS
14 grams low-fire silver clay
Syringe clay with medium tip
Pill bottle (or other small jar)
Nonstick sheet
Clear tape
Self-sealing plastic wrap
Items to be embedded
Cotton swabs
¾-in. (19 mm) square cutter (optional)
Metal clay extruder (optional)

TOOL KITS
Wet-clay tool kit
Greenware tool kit
Finishing tool kit
UV-cure resin kit (see p. 106)

Firing Schedule LOW-FIRE
Butane torch, gas stovetop, or kiln

1 Tape a small piece of nonstick sheet around the bottle. (Our jar of ACS Overlay Paste was just the right size.)

2 Create the round frame, either by extruding clay or rolling it.

To extrude: Roll 14 grams of clay between your fingers to fit the extruder tube, insert the clay, and quickly cap the extruder. Extrude the entire amount of clay onto the nonstick surface [A]. Cover the clay with a damp paper towel and immediately clean out any clay that remains in the extruder, saving it for later use.

To roll: Using 1.5 mm slats/6 cards and the roller, roll 14 grams of clay into a strip about 5/16 in. (8 mm) wide and 4 in. (10 cm) long. Use a tissue blade to trim to ¼ in. (7 mm) wide. Cover any leftover clay with a moist paper towel.

3 Wrap the clay strip around the base of the pill bottle [B]. With the craft knife, make an angled cut where the ends overlap and push the ends gently together [C]. Add syringe clay to reinforce the seam. Smooth the clay with a moist paintbrush.

4 Let dry until the ring holds its shape. Remove the ring from the bottle so it can continue to dry (and shrink slightly) without pulling the seam apart.

5 Refine the seam, adding syringe clay if necessary. Let dry. Sand until no trace of a seam remains.

6 To make the bail, roll the remaining clay to 1 mm/4 cards thick and use a craft knife or the square cutter to cut a ¾-in. square of clay [D]. Wrap the clay around a narrow straw or bamboo skewer as shown [E]. Leave the bail on the straw to dry completely.

Many photos and computer prints are UV-sensitive and may fade when exposed to the resin-curing lamp. Never use a treasured original image! Scan it and make extra prints to test.

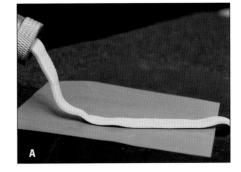

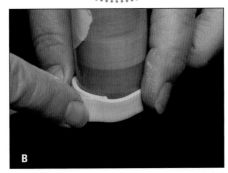

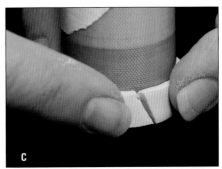

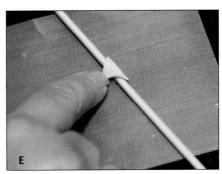

A jewelry bail allows a pendant to hang from a chain or cord. Bails come in many forms, from a simple loop to a more elaborate design (like this one).

7 Sand the bail until smooth. Use syringe clay to attach the bail to the frame, smoothing the join with a damp paintbrush **[F]**. Let dry completely. Sand the join until smooth.

8 Fire the frame following the low-fire schedule. Let cool (the frame can be quenched for quicker cooling if desired).

9 For a matte finish, brush the outside of the pendant with a stainless steel or brass brush. For a mirror finish, use an agate burnisher, wet/dry sandpapers, or polishing papers. Do not brush, sand, or burnish the inside of the frame; a rough surface will help the resin adhere.

10 Set up the UV-cure or halogen lamp. To prepare the frame for the resin, attach a piece of self-sealing plastic wrap across the back of the frame **[G]**. (Wide packing tape works too.) Press to seal it to the frame. Turn the frame right side up and burnish the back against the table for a tight seal.

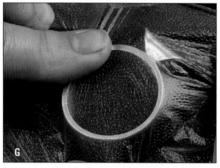

11 With the piece right side up, use a toothpick to drop resin into the well, creating a shallow base layer at the back of the frame **[H]**. Remove any bubbles by heating the resin for a second or two with the butane lighter. The resin is not flammable, but be careful not to melt the plastic wrap. Cure the resin by placing it under the lamp; UV lamps cure the resin in approximately 2 minutes; halogen lamps may take up to 10 minutes. You can't overcure the resin, but once it sets, it can't be undone.

12 Plan your layers, working from back to front and keeping in mind the depth of the frame. You don't want anything sticking out of the resin. Using the tweezers, add a layer of items to be trapped within the resin. Add another layer of resin **[I]**. Remove any air bubbles with the lighter, being careful not to singe embedded items. Cure the resin under the lamp. Repeat until all items are embedded and apply a final layer of resin. It's OK if this layer domes slightly higher than the silver frame.

13 Use a cotton swab and resin gel cleanser to clean the surface of the resin. Remove the plastic backing from the frame. If desired, add a layer of resin to the back, cure the layer, and clean it.

14 String the pendant on a chain or cord.

Once you get the hang of it, you might enjoy making square resin-filled pendants too.

You'll find more tips and tricks for working with UV-cure resin gel on p. 106.

To the Moon!
embellished photo frame

Photographs capture our favorite moments and allow us to remember and relive them each time we catch a glimpse. Wouldn't you love to find the perfect frame to fit your sweet memories? In this project, we show you how to take an ordinary picture frame and make it extraordinary—perfect for precious moments and fitting any room décor.

Choose an all-ceramic frame so you can kiln-fire it after adding outlines in silver. The space-themed embellishments have a playful, coloring-book style created with the vibrant colors of UV-cure resin.

quick reference

MATERIALS & TOOLS
Low-fire syringe clay with large tip
ACS Overlay Paste
Ceramic photo frame
Plastic glitter star
Isopropyl alcohol
Cotton swabs
Epoxy
Binder clips

TOOL KITS
Wet-clay tool kit
Greenware tool kit
Finishing tool kit
UV-cure resin kit (see p. 106)

Firing Schedule
CERAMICS WITH OVERLAY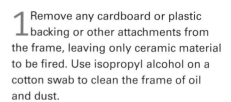
Kiln only; slow ramp. See details on
p. 101.

1 Remove any cardboard or plastic backing or other attachments from the frame, leaving only ceramic material to be fired. Use isopropyl alcohol on a cotton swab to clean the frame of oil and dust.

2 Plan your designs by drawing freehand sketches or using copyright-free art **[A]**.

3 Paint a thick base of Overlay Paste wherever you plan to add a design in syringe clay. You can choose whether you want to make an outline with the paste **[B]** or if you'd prefer a solid silver background behind the designs. Let the paste dry completely.

4 Trace the outlines of the designs with syringe clay **[C]**. Use a moist paintbrush to tap and smooth the syringe clay lines, making sure they are well connected to each other and to the paste base.

5 Let the syringe clay dry thoroughly. If necessary, scratch away extra Overlay Paste with a toothpick **[D]**.

A

B

C

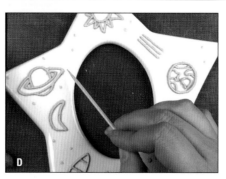

D

Overlay Paste is the silver "glue" that will allow the syringe clay to adhere to the frame.

6 Fire the frame in a programmable kiln, following the Ceramics With Overlay schedule. Let the kiln come back to room temperature on its own before opening it.

7 Burnish the tops and outsides of the silver syringe lines [E]. Do not burnish inside the lines.

8 With toothpicks, draw UV resin gel from the container and place it on the glass square or ceramic tile, where you will mix the resin with color. Mix tiny amounts of dye—less than one drop at a time—into the resin to create the colors you want [F]. The resin will remain workable until cured as long as you are away from windows or any lights that contain UV rays.

9 Use toothpicks to place the colored resin into the silver outlines [G]. Let the resin level for a few moments.

While working with the UV-cure resin gel, avoid sunlight and halogen lamps—or any other lamp that contains UV light— so the resin doesn't cure before you're ready. If you're sure your lighting is free of UV rays, you can mix multiple colors before you begin dropping them into place.

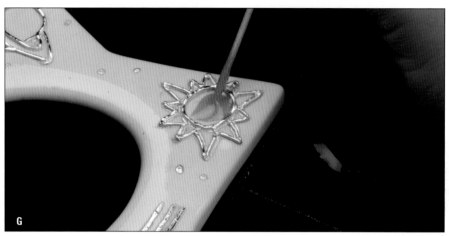

SILVER PLUS

Seascape variation

Molded silver shapes decorate this frame. First we made molds from actual shells with two-part molding compound and found some candy molds in other seaworthy shapes. We used lump clay to form the shapes and then fired them. We used Overlay Paste to add "seaweed" detail and to fuse the shapes to the frame in a second firing. Once cool, we brushed and burnished the silver, then added real shells to the frame with epoxy.

You could simplify this variation for a glass, plastic, or any other frame that isn't ceramic and therefore not fireable—make the silver elements separately with low-fire lump clay, fire them, and attach them to the frame with epoxy.

10 If you see any bubbles in the gel, use the butane lighter or a hair dryer on "hot" to zap the resin with a burst of heat [H]. This releases the trapped air. This takes only a second or two; be careful not to singe your fingers or the frame. Fill each outlined shape with resin nearly to the top of the silver.

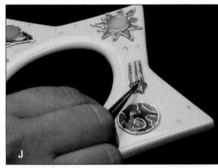

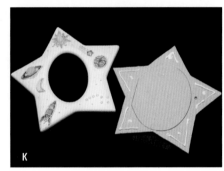

11 As you finish filling a shape, cure it under the UV-cure or halogen lamp, following the directions in the resin gel packaging [I].

12 Repeat steps 10–11 until all the designs are filled with cured resin. For a final touch, we used epoxy to attach a plastic glitter star [J].

13 Use the cleanser to remove the sticky top layer of the resin.

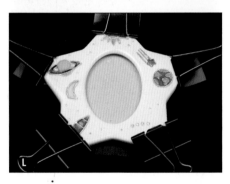

14 Reattach the frame backing. You may need to use epoxy to glue it back together; if so, take care not to glue shut the "door" for inserting photographs [K]. Binder clips will keep the backing flush against the frame while the epoxy dries [L]. Place a favorite photo inside the frame.

Silver Couture
cuff links

Cuff links are a nice complement to a business or formal shirt. Even guys who claim they never wear jewelry can accessorize with and appreciate an elegant or sporty pair of cuff links.

Cuff links are made in the same way you'd make a tie tack, pendant, or toggle clasp, with the addition of either a bar or a chain to go through the buttonholes. In this project, each cuff link has two identical "faces" linked by jump rings. They're so easy to make, we show a matching tie tack as well (see Not So Tacky project, p. 62).

quick reference

MATERIALS & TOOLS
14–20 grams of low-fire silver clay
Low-fire paste clay
4 fine silver screw eyes
12 10 mm jump rings
Texture stamp
ACS Overlay Paste (optional)
ACS Gold Paste Clay (optional)

TOOL KITS
Wet-clay tool kit
Greenware tool kit
Finishing tool kit
Jewelry assembly kit

Firing Schedule LOW-FIRE
Butane torch, gas stovetop, or kiln

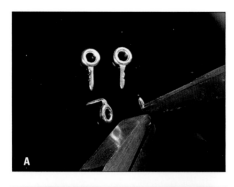

1 Using jewelry pliers, bend the notched shanks of the screw eyes at a 90-degree angle [A].

2 Roll the clay to 2 mm/8 cards [B].

3 Roll the texture onto the clay [C]. Consider deepening or enhancing the texture with a needle tool [D].

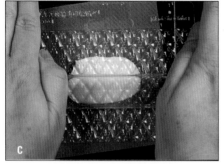

4 Use the tissue blade or a craft knife to trim the cuff link panel [E]. (We designed ours so we could cut multiple panels from the same roll of clay [F].)

5 Flip the panel over, being careful not to distort the texture on the front. Grasp the screw eye with jewelry pliers and embed the shank into the back of the panel [G]. Insert the screw eye as though you are inserting a key into a hole, making one neat, angled hole [H].

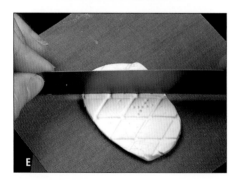

6 Add paste clay around the screw eye to ensure a strong attachment and to cover any indentations made when you inserted the screw eye [I].

7 Repeat steps 5–6 with the other panel.

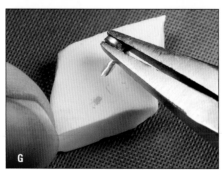

8 Dry the pieces completely. (Continued handling of the wet pieces may work the screw eye loose.)

9 Use sanding sticks or mini files to smooth any lumps around the screw eyes **[J]**. Bevel the sides of the panels, removing any sharp edges **[K]**.

10 Use polishing papers or sanding pads to smooth the panel fronts.

11 Fire the pieces following the low-fire schedule.

12 If you would like to add gold to the cuff links, do it before the pieces are brushed or burnished. Add a coat of Overlay Paste to the area where you plan to add gold. Let dry. Apply three thin layers of gold paste clay to the panel fronts, drying completely between layers **[L]**. Fire the pieces according to the manufacturer's instructions for gold paste. Let the pieces to come to room temperature naturally.

13 Burnish the pieces with an agate burnisher to raise a shiny luster **[M]**. (Tumbling fired gold paste isn't recommended, as the gold may begin to come off.)

14 We used a little bit of chain maille technique to link the cuff link panels. To start, close two jump rings.

15 Open a jump ring and pick up the two closed rings. Close the jump ring.

16 Repeat step 15. (You have created a 2-by-2 link chain.) Open a jump ring, and pick up two end links of chain and the loop of a cuff link. Close the ring. Repeat on the other end **[N]**. Attach the cuff links to your guy of choice!

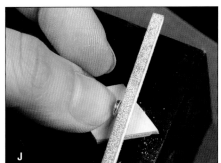

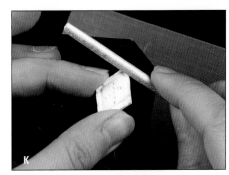

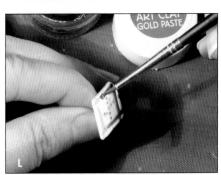

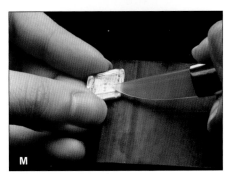

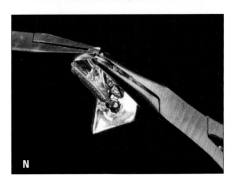

These cuff links were molded from football-shaped buttons.

PL8 4U

mini vanity plate

In our search to identify ourselves as individuals, no space goes overlooked. Even our license plates have potential as traveling billboards for our ideals or preferences. License plates describe everything from pet friendliness (IM4DOGS) or food likes and dislikes (T8R H8R). When applying for real vanity plates, we're limited by the watchful eye of the DMV and whether our catchy phrase is already in use, among other things. In our version, nothing is taboo. Feel free to go as wild or as detailed as you'd like.

quick reference

MATERIALS & TOOLS
20 grams low-fire silver clay
Photopolymer plate of license
   plate art (see sidebar and p. 104)
2 6 mm jump rings
Syringe clay (optional)
Pebeo Vitrea 160 paints (optional)

TOOL KITS
Wet-clay tool kit
Greenware tool kit
Polishing tools
Jewelry assembly kit

Firing Schedule LOW-FIRE
Kiln recommended, but may be fired with torch or on stovetop. Kiln-firing is best because you can weight the plate during firing to prevent warping.

Tips for creating the license plate art

Before you start this project, you'll need to make photopolymer plates of a license plate. Find an image of a state plate you like. If you're handy with photo-editing software, use it to remove unwanted parts, and create a high-contrast image about 2½ in. (64 mm) wide. (To work by hand, print or photocopy the image to size and trace the state name and other details of the plate onto the transparency film.) Leave the center open so you can add letters and/or numbers in a later step.

Make two copies of your finished art on transparency film and sandwich them; this nice, solid black makes the best photopolymer plate. See p. 104 for complete instructions.

See p. 104 for complete instructions.

1 Roll the clay to 2 mm/8 cards thick and slightly larger than the photopolymer plate **[A]**.

2 Press the plate evenly and firmly into the clay. You'll see the clay pressing into the clear areas **[B]**.

3 Use a tissue blade to trim the four sides of the clay image **[C]**.

4 Use a narrow straw to punch holes in the upper left and right corners at least 2 mm from the edges **[D]**.

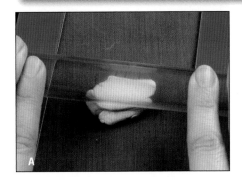

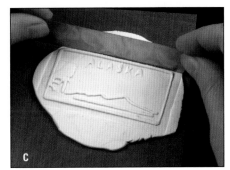

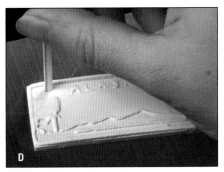

SILVER PLUS

5 You can scribe letters into the clay with a needle tool **[E]**, or you can use syringe clay to create raised lettering. If using syringe clay, pat the letters down with a moist paintbrush to firmly adhere them to the clay base.

6 Dry completely. Since this piece is prone to warping, we recommend slow air-drying at least overnight. If you want to dry the clay more quickly using a drying appliance, keep a close eye on it and flip it over at any sign of warping.

7 Sand the back and sides of the plate smooth, removing any sharp edges or corners **[F]**. Carefully smooth any rough edges around the lettering.

8 Fire the piece following the low-fire schedule. To weight the piece to help prevent warping, place the piece on fiber board, add a layer of fiber blanket, and another piece of fiber board on top. Allow to cool (this piece may be quenched to cool quickly if desired).

> If you're going for an authentic license plate look, use only 7 or 8 characters, with a mix of letters and numbers.

9 Brush with a brass or stainless steel brush **[G]**. If you prefer a shiny finish, tumble-polish or burnish with an agate burnisher.

10 If desired, add a patina with liver of sulfur. You can apply the patina to certain areas of the plate with a cotton swab, darkening designs or letters without coloring the rest of the plate.

2CRE8 Color

This mini plate shows how we added color to the silver using Pebeo Vitrea 160, a water-soluble, enamel-like paint (see p. 106 for more details on Vitrea paints). Once dried overnight and cured in your home oven, the color is permanent.

11 Use silver polish and a polishing cloth to shine the plate, being careful not to remove any color achieved with the patina **[H]**.

12 Attach the jump rings to the hanging holes **[I]**. Consider hanging the mini plate from a decorative cord that matches the color of the recipient's vehicle.

Fistful of Dollars
money clip

Personalized money clips make cool gifts—especially when your guy is into something off the beaten path. To show you how versatile silver clay can be, we designed this money clip to pay homage to our favorite Clint Eastwood movie.

In this project, you'll fuse a fired, silver clay front to a sterling silver clip using ACS Overlay Paste. You'll need to do a little bit of sculpting to create the project as shown. If you'd like to make a easier version, skip the fist and make a simple shape (like a heart, a dollar sign, or both!) to layer over the purchased clip.

quick reference

MATERIALS & TOOLS
Solid sterling silver money clip
15 grams low-fire silver clay
Paste clay
ACS Overlay Paste
Dollar-sign stamp (from an alphabet set)
Isopropyl alcohol
Two large binder clips
Sheet of ceramic fiber paper
Fine metalworking file

TOOL KITS
Wet-clay tool kit
Greenware tool kit
Finishing tool kit

Firing Schedule LOW-FIRE
Kiln only; see p. 79 for details

Our money clip base is from Rio Grande (see p. 107). The back is solid and the front has a large cutout. Be sure your clip base is solid sterling silver, not silver plated; plating could come off during firing.

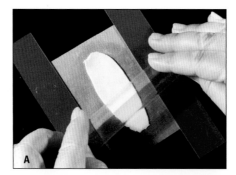

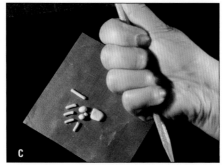

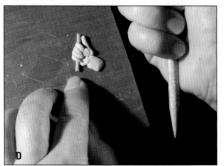

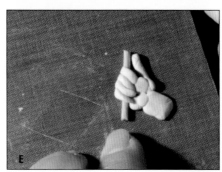

Practice your sculpting skills with some polymer clay before opening the silver clay.

1 Roll 10 grams of silver clay to a thickness of 1 mm/4 cards **[A]**.

2 Trim the silver clay to be 1 mm larger on all sides than the front of the clip base **[B]**. This will allow for 8–10% shrinkage of the clay during firing. Air-drying almost always guarantees that a flat piece won't curl, so set the panel aside to air dry. No need to dry it quickly—you'll be busy sculpting for a few minutes!

3 We used Judi's fist as a model and planned our rough shapes: three balls, four short sticks, one longer stick, and a flat square **[C]**. Although the size will vary a bit depending on the size of your money clip, these are the shapes you'll make with the silver clay.

4 Assemble your hand sections as shown. Squish together three small balls for the palm, and rest the ends of the "fingers" on the palm **[D]**. Insert a small piece of toothpick under the four "fingers" to hold them up as you begin your sculpting, and rest the "thumb" against the toothpick **[E]**. Don't be afraid to use your own hand as a reference! Cover your clay with a damp paper towel, and let the clay absorb moisture for a few minutes.

5 Use sculpting tools to round up the two fleshy pads at the base of the palm, add wrinkles at the wrist and at the finger and thumb joints, and don't forget the fingernails (somehow fingernails add that final touch that says, "Hey! This is a hand!") **[F]**. Notice that we trimmed the "wrist" to be at the correct angle to fit on the flat panel we cut in step 2; place the "hand" onto the panel before you cut it to be sure the size and angle are correct. Set aside to dry.

6 To make the dollars, roll a small amount of clay and cut a ¾-in. (19 mm) square. Use the dollar-sign stamp (from an alphabet set) to mark the edges of the bills; if you can't find (or carve) a stamp this small, scribe the "$" symbol into the clay with a toothpick **[G]**. Gently bunch or fanfold the piece, then cut it in half across the middle as shown. These dollars will extend above and below the fist.

7 Using paste clay, paste the dollars to the fist **[H]**. Dry completely.

8 Using paste clay, securely attach the dried fistful of dollars to the front panel. To create the stack of coins, roll a short snake of silver clay. Cut it in half lengthwise, and attach the flat side to the bottom of the panel with paste. Using sculpting tools and a craft knife, cut lines to simulate stacked coins **[I]**. Add a flat coin or two at the bottom or top. Mark coin faces with the dollar sign stamp.

9 Dry the entire front panel until it's bone dry. Use sandpaper to groom all of the edges of the front piece and any rough edges on the sculpted hand.

10 Cover the piece with fiber blanket, and gently add a piece of fire brick to help keep the piece flat during kiln-firing. Fusing to the base will be easier if the piece doesn't warp or curl. Fire according to the low-fire schedule.

11 Does your front panel fit the base **[J]**? If it's too large, file the sides until they fit. If the piece is narrower than the clip blank, fill in the gaps with Overlay Paste prior to the second firing.

12 Hold the pieces together and look at them from the side to make certain that the top panel is flat against the clip base **[K]**. If it's not flat, use flatnose pliers to gently flex the

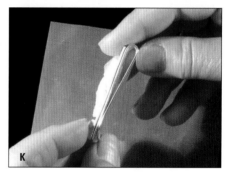

Oxidation 101

One of many things we like about silver clay is that its 99.9% pure silver content means that it's slow to tarnish and doesn't get nasty discoloration during firing due to oxidation. Heating a copper-bearing alloy like the sterling silver clip base in the presence of oxygen can create unwanted surface oxides or possibly the deeper, more insidious oxides called firescale.

You don't have to worry about oxidation on the sculpted front, but to avoid it on the sterling silver, here's what you'll do:

First, fire the sculpted silver clay alone. When it's cool, apply Overlay Paste to attach it to the sterling silver base, let it dry, and fire the piece again (both firings follow the low-fire schedule). When the piece is cool, if you notice any oxidation on the sterling silver base, fill a jelly jar with white vinegar, place it on a mug warmer, and soak for four hours. The mild acid should help dissolve the oxides. Rinse. Wet-sand any discoloration that remains. Finish with a silver-polish buffing.

front piece ever so slightly so it is flat **[L]**. Remember that fired silver clay is not super-flexible; if you bend it too far, it can snap, and you'll have to repair it before proceeding.

13 Score the surface of the clip with the metalworking file **[M]**. This gives the silver clay paste a good surface to grip as it fuses to the sterling.

14 Clean the scored surface of the blank clip with alcohol. Let it dry thoroughly, then apply a generous layer of Overlay Paste **[N]**. Quickly position the front piece on the clip base and squeeze tightly, until the paste squeezes out the sides. Dry completely; preferably under pressure from metal binder clips on both ends of the clip, exerting even pressure across the entire face of the clip.

15 Fill the edges with additional layers of Overlay Paste **[O]**. Dry thoroughly between coats, repeating until the seams are filled.

16 Sand the seams until smooth **[P]**.

17 Once the joined pieces are completely smoothed, we inserted a folded sheet of ceramic fiber paper into the money clip before kiln-firing **[Q]**.

18 Fire the piece a second time following the low-fire schedule. Tumble for two hours if desired.

19 If you want to add patina, clean the piece with wet baking soda paste and rinse. Apply liver of sulfur solution sparingly using a cotton swab **[R]**. Often you can achieve a gold color (nice for the coins) by leaving the solution on the surface of the silver for just a few seconds and then rinsing it in cool water.

20 Brush or polish to remove some of the patina and add highlights **[S]**.

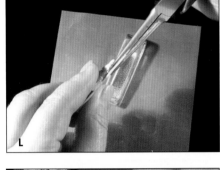

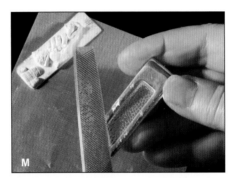

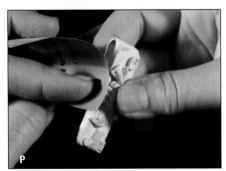

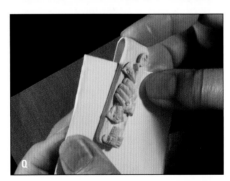

About ceramic fiber paper

Ceramic fiber paper is interesting stuff; it's actually spun ceramic, and although it will blacken when kiln-fired, it's able to withstand the heat well enough to provide a thin barrier between the two silver surfaces. If a drop or two of Overlay Paste happens to get within the clip, the fiber paper will keep it from fusing shut.

4 Silver On Ceramics

Silver Savings
painted piggy bank

Every kid should have a piggy bank. This personalized piggy makes it fun for children to start practicing good saving habits early in life.

We modeled our lettering for Ollie on a favorite plaid blanket. Follow our design, or enjoy improvising your own with the child's name, room theme, favorite colors, or beloved characters.

quick reference

MATERIALS & TOOLS
ACS Overlay Paste
Ceramic piggy bank
Isopropyl alcohol
Paper towels
Cotton swabs
Fine-tip paintbrush
Pebeo Vitrea 160 paints

TOOL KIT
Finishing tool kit

Firing Schedule
CERAMICS WITH OVERLAY
Kiln only; slow ramp. See details on p. 101.

1 Measure the area available on the piggy bank's side. Plan the letters of the name you've chosen by drawing them freehand on a sheet of paper or creating a pattern with computer lettering to fit the available area [A].

2 Remove any plastic stopper or felt feet that the piggy bank might have. Clean the bank and the palms of your hands with isopropyl alcohol to remove dust, dirt, and oils.

3 Using the Overlay Paste cap as a cup, dilute a small amount of paste with water to the consistency of milk. Using a fine-tip paintbrush, outline letters [B], then add interior lines (such as plaid stripes) or other decoration to the bank [C].

4 Let the silver paste dry completely. Use a toothpick to scratch away any stray silver.

5 Fire the bank in a programmable kiln following the Ceramics With Overlay schedule.

6 Use an agate burnisher to shine the silver [D].

7 Using a clean, fine-tip paintbrush, apply paint colors as desired [E]. Let dry at room temperature for 24 hours.

8 To cure the paint, place the bank in a regular oven [F] for the recommended time and temperature, usually about 35 minutes at 300°F (150°C.)

For extra luck and good fortune, include a deposit toward a college fund inside the gift piggy!

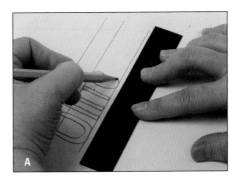

Sgraffito fun

This variation was created with sgraffito, a scratch-away technique, using a coloring book page for reference. Judi's husband made this playful piggy. For other examples of sgraffito, see the What a Treat! project (p. 91), the Family Tree project (p. 94), and the Gallery (p. 98).

Fancy Flowers
customized flowerpot

Ideal for friends, relatives, teachers, colleagues, or neighbors, this simple project is elegant and inexpensive. Offer it as a quick "Thanks!" for the homegrown tomatoes you've received over the years or give it as a meaningful gesture of appreciation to someone who has a talent for nurturing. We offer directions for a stenciled version (shown above) or one that shows off a youngster's handprints (see p. 86).

Choosing a ceramic pot

Pots in darker colors show off the silver detailing the best. When you choose your pot, make sure it doesn't have any internal cracks, which could cause breakage during firing as the material expands and contracts. The easiest way to determine this is to place the pot on a hard surface, like a countertop, and tap it lightly with a spoon. A pot that is sound will usually produce a bell-like tone, like "tink," when tapped. A pot that has internal fractures (they may not be visible to the naked eye) will make a flatter sound, more like "thunk." As a general rule, most sound stoneware pots will hold up well to refiring, but even thinner pots, such as slip cast porcelain, fire well if handled correctly.

This technique can be used to make other gifts as well, such as a casserole dish or a fruit bowl. (If you're buying a pot directly from the maker, ask whether the glaze is food-safe.) Ceramics that you decorate with silver can be used in the oven but not in a microwave, and we recommend hand washing.

quick reference

MATERIALS & TOOLS
ACS Overlay Paste
Glazed flowerpot
Self-stick stencils or child's hands
Isopropyl alcohol
Paper towels
Cotton swabs
Fine-tip paintbrush
Pipette or small spoon (optional)

TOOL KIT
Finishing tool kit

Firing Schedule
CERAMICS WITH OVERLAY
Kiln only; slow ramp. See details on p. 101.

*After you've **removed** a silver-enhanced glazed ceramic item from the kiln, you may hear pinging sounds coming from it—that's the glaze cooling and is normal.*

1 Clean the surface of the flowerpot with isopropyl alcohol.

2 If you're creating a stenciled design, position all of the self-stick stencils on the flowerpot **[A]**.

3 Apply Overlay Paste to the open areas of the stencils with the tip of the paintbrush, filling them evenly **[B]**.

4 Dry the paste completely at room temperature. It dries quickly, but be sure that it is completely dry before moving on. You'll be able to tell because there will be no "dark patches" on the clay—Overlay Paste lightens considerably as it dries.

5 When the paste is bone dry, peel the stencils from the flowerpot **[C]**.

This flowerpot would be beautiful as part of an indoor garden or would be equally lovely outdoors.

SILVER ON CERAMICS

Handprint version: Thin the Overlay Paste to the consistency of milk, using a pipette or small spoon to add only a drop of water at a time **[D]**. Use the paintbrush to smear a juicy coat of the diluted paste onto the child's palms **[E]**. Allow the child to grab the flowerpot, or help roll a hand across the surface of the pottery **[F]**.

To clean up the handprints, dab a moist paper towel at the edges of the impression. If the print is smeared beyond repair, simply wipe the surface clean and try again. When all handprints are satisfactory, wipe the handprint hero's hands clean.

6 Use a toothpick to scratch away any excess paste. If desired, paint a name on the flowerpot and allow to dry completely **[G]**.

7 Clean between and around the silver with alcohol to remove any stray silver that might fuse to the pot and create a "hazy" look post-firing.

8 Fire the flowerpot according to the Ceramics With Overlay schedule.

9 Use an agate burnisher to shine the silver, then polish with jewelry polish and a soft cloth.

Overlay Paste is certified nontoxic, so even if your little volunteer tries to lick a finger before you can wipe up, no worries.

A gift of green
Consider planting flowers or herbs in the pot before presenting your gift to a deserving parent, grandparent, neighbor, teacher, or gardener.

Be forewarned: We've found that tiny tots either love or really dislike the feeling of wet clay on their grabbers!

Grandma's going to love this!

Sip in Silver
personalized drinkware

Coffee, hot tea, or cocoa in a unique mug can make a chilly day special. In this project, you'll personalize a pair of ceramic mugs with the recipients' names and use a stamp to create a pattern. Consider using symbols with significance to the couple. The mugs are perfect for a wedding or anniversary gift.

Let the gift recipients know that they should not put the mugs in the microwave. The silver accents are real metal and can burn or melt and may cause damage to the microwave.

quick reference

MATERIALS & TOOLS
ACS Overlay Paste
Matching set of ceramic mugs
Isopropyl alcohol
Paper towels
Cotton swabs
Painter's tape
Foam-backed stamps
Fine-tip paintbrush
Pipette or small spoon
Toothpicks

TOOL KIT
Finishing tool kit

Firing Schedule
CERAMICS WITH OVERLAY
Kiln only; slow ramp. See details on p. 101.

A

B

C

D

E

F

G

1 Use painter's tape to mask the mug's top and bottom (or any other area) where you don't want the silver design to appear **[A]**. Clean the surface of the mug with isopropyl alcohol.

2 Using the cap as a cup, dilute some Overlay Paste with water until it's the consistency of milk. Using the fine-tip paintbrush, paint a name on the mug in paste **[B]**.

3 Paint a thick layer of paste onto the raised areas of the stamp **[C]**. Press the stamp onto the mug in a rolling motion **[D]**. (If the design smears a bit, don't worry—you can clean it up in a later step.) Fill the space with pattern.

4 Allow the silver to dry completely, then use a toothpick to scratch away any misplaced silver. Remove the tape from the mug **[E]**.

5 Clean the areas around the silver with alcohol to remove any stray silver dust, avoiding the silver design.

6 Repeat steps 1–5 to create a second decorated mug.

7 Fire the mugs following the Ceramics With Overlay schedule.

8 If you want the silver shiny, use an agate burnisher **[F]**, and shine with a bit of jewelry polish on a cloth.

9 If the mugs are light-colored, consider adding patina to the silver with a liver of sulfur solution **[G]**.

Perfect presentation

Fill the cups with a favorite tea blend, coffee beans, or candy. Create a little tag that tells how you made these personalized mugs and reminds them not to put their sip-ware in the microwave! Washing by hand is also recommended.

We used kanji characters to decorate this pair of goblets.

Let Them Eat Cake
inscribed server

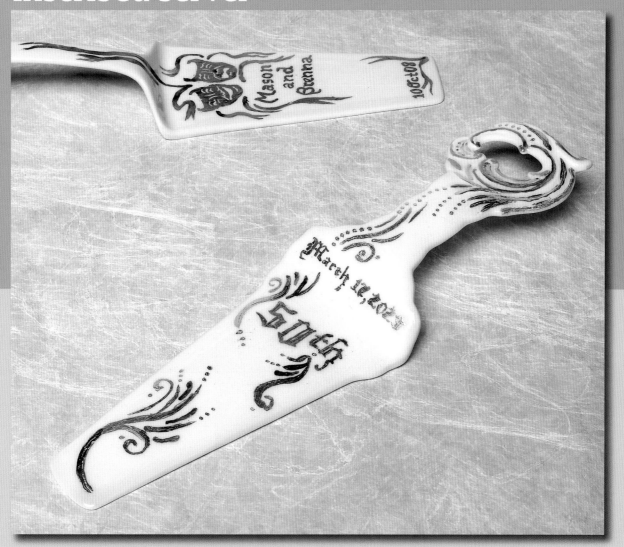

Cutting the cake at a wedding has become a frosting-filled tradition for newly married couples. Often special cake servers have been purchased for the event—functional tools that will be treasured for a lifetime. These personalized servers also make a sweet gift for anniversaries, housewarmings, birthdays, or graduation celebrations.

Use paste clay to paint the lettering onto the server. You can use silver, gold, or both—just follow the appropriate firing schedule. If you combine, follow the schedule for gold.

quick reference

MATERIALS & TOOLS
ACS Overlay Paste
Gold paste clay (optional)
Ceramic cake server
Isopropyl alcohol
Paper towels
Cotton swabs
Computer print of lettering
Fine-tip paintbrush
Toothpicks

TOOL KIT
Finishing tool kit

Firing Schedule
CERAMICS WITH OVERLAY
Kiln only; slow ramp. See details on p. 101.

A

B

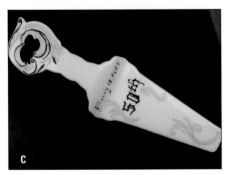

C

D

1 Clean the entire surface area of the server with isopropyl alcohol **[A]**.

2 Following your lettering guide, paint Overlay Paste onto the server with the fine-tip paintbrush **[B]**. Accent with gold paste, if desired.

3 Allow the paste to dry completely. Apply a second coat, if desired, and add other details by painting either silver or gold paste. Let dry completely **[C]**. The dried paste will look flat and dull; resist the urge to buff or sand at this stage! The paste is thin and delicate, and may flake or rub off.

4 Scratch off any out-of-place dried paste with a toothpick. Clean any undecorated areas with alcohol.

5 Fire using a slow ramp. If gold was used, follow the hold schedule for gold; otherwise follow the Ceramics With Overlay schedule.

6 Burnish the metal with an agate burnisher **[D]** and shine with jewelry polish and a soft cloth.

The cake server will be food safe but should be washed by hand.

What a Treat!
embellished canister

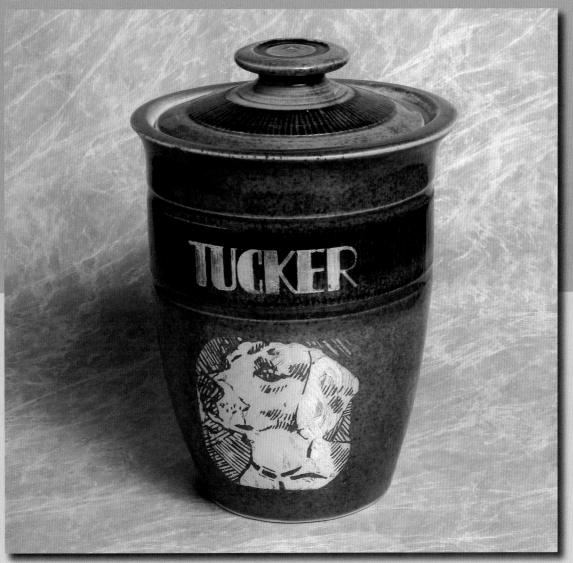

We love to love our pets. They're always happy to see us, they love us unconditionally, and they never talk back. Doesn't your unwavering buddy deserve a personalized treat jar?

In this project, we'll show you how to transfer a picture of your pet to the canister using the technique of *sgraffito*, which means "to scratch off." Sgraffito is a marvelous technique because you don't have to have one iota of drawing skill to make a perfect image!

**It's always
a good idea** to use a
separate container,
such as the lid of the
Overlay Paste jar, as
a cup for diluting
your paste.

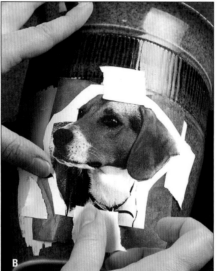

Pet imagery

**If your favorite photograph is
in color, use your computer's
photo-editing software to
convert it to grayscale and size
it to fit the canister. (Converting
the image to grayscale will help
you see the contrast better
for the sgraffito process.) Or
simply make a black-and-white
photocopy to the right size at
your local library or copy shop.**

1 Use isopropyl alcohol to clean the
surface where you'll be adding
silver, including the lid. If your treat jar
has rubber or cork pads on the bottom,
remove them so they do not burn away
in the kiln. Burning rubber will smell truly
awful and set off your smoke alarm!

2 Use the pipette or small spoon to
add a drop of water at a time until
the Overlay Paste is the consistency of
milk. Don't over-dilute; a little water goes
a long way. Spread the paste across an
area slightly larger than your image **[A]**.
Dry completely.

3 Place the transfer paper over the
paste layer, then put the image
on top. Tape the paper securely to the
canister so it doesn't shift while you're
working **[B]**.

4 Use the pencil to transfer outlines
of the image to the silver. Trace
around the eyes, the head, the nose, etc.
Try to capture what makes the animal
unique—the tilt of the head or ear, the
spots or dark colors in the fur. Remove
the transfer paper and image **[C]**.

5 Using a toothpick (or other wooden tool), begin removing lines and areas you transferred **[D]**. Scratch away additional lines or patterns to give more dimension to the image **[E]**. Remember, any dust scratched off is reusable, so keep all that fallen powder and return it to your Overlay Paste jar.

6 Add the pet's name to the jar with Overlay Paste **[F]**, either near the picture or on the lid. The name can be added freehand, or you can use the same sgraffito technique with some printed lettering. (It can be helpful to apply straight lines of masking tape as lettering guides—that helped us keep the blocky "Tucker" lettering in line.) Dry the paste completely, then clean around the silver with alcohol to prevent any stray dust from fusing.

7 Fire according to the Ceramics With Overlay schedule.

8 Burnish the silver with the agate burnisher **[G]**. Shine with jewelry polish and a soft cloth.

> **Fill the jar** with tasty treats before presenting it to its new owner.

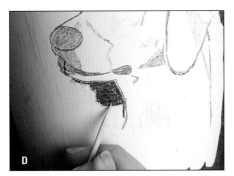

Silver bones

This variation was decorated with low-fire silver clay dog bones. We used the mold shown in the pet tag project (p. 39) as well as a scrapbooking punch to create the shapes, attached them to the canister with Overlay Paste, and fired the canister according to the Ceramics With Overlay schedule.

Family Tree
decorated plate

A family tree and its branches represent the connection of each member to the family as a whole. In this version of a family tree, individuals are represented by their birthstones (fireable CZs), placed decoratively around the tree. Consider leaving space for additional family members—you can add more CZs later and refire the plate.

To get started, look for an image of a tree without leaves. Use one of our patterns (see p. 100) or work from a photograph and draw your own. The silver tree is created with a scratch-away technique called *sgraffito*.

see p. 100

quick reference

MATERIALS & TOOLS
ACS Overlay Paste
Low-fire syringe clay with medium tip
Glazed ceramic plate
3 mm CZs (a birthstone for each person)
Isopropyl alcohol
Paper towels
Cotton swabs
Pipette or small spoon
Fine-tip and medium-tip paintbrush
Tweezers
Tree image sized to fit plate

Family name lettering reference
Transfer paper (carbon or graphite)
Clear tape

TOOL KIT
Finishing tool kit

Firing Schedule
CERAMICS WITH OVERLAY
Kiln only; slow ramp. See details on p. 101.

See details on p. 101.

1 Clean the surface of the plate well with isopropyl alcohol.

2 Dilute the Overlay Paste by adding water, a drop at a time, until the paste is the consistency of milk. With a medium-tip paintbrush, spread a layer of paste on the plate over an area slightly larger than the image of the tree [A]. Let dry completely.

3 Place the transfer paper over the dried paste, and place the tree image over the paper. Tape the sheets to the plate so they do not move while you trace. Using light pressure, trace the tree outline with a pencil [B].

4 Lift the papers from the plate [C]. Check that you have captured the entire tree image. If you'd like to add any branches, sketch them gently with pencil.

5 Use a toothpick or bamboo skewer to scratch away any paste that is not part of the tree design [D]. Don't use anything sharp, such as a craft knife, to scratch off dried paste; the blade might scratch the glaze on the plate, creating unwanted silver lines in the scratches after firing. Use a dry medium-tip paintbrush to move all of the loose silver dust aside as you work. Return the silver dust to the Overlay Paste jar.

6 Check the silver image of the tree to be sure that no branches have been scratched away by mistake. Add any missing elements with the fine-tip paintbrush and paste [E].

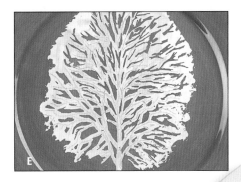

You'll find a list of birthstones on p. 101.

This variation uses patina on the silver for high contrast.

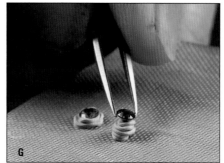

7 Form the bezels for the CZs: On the nonstick surface, make several layers of syringe-clay rings slightly larger than the CZ **[F]**. Use tweezers to pick up a CZ and place it in the center of the setting **[G]**. Push the stone into the setting until the table is even with the top of the rings. Set a CZ for each family member. Dry all the settings completely.

8 Plan the placement of the CZs on the silver tree. Put a drop of Overlay Paste on the tree, and use tweezers to place a CZ in its setting onto the drop of wet paste **[H]**. Dry thoroughly.

9 Clean the area below the tree with isopropyl alcohol. Apply an area of Overlay Paste slightly larger than the name area. Transfer the family name lettering **[I]**. Using the sgraffito technique, remove all of the paste except the lettering. Dry the lettering completely, scratching off excess clay if needed.

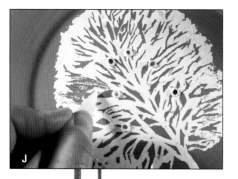

> **Brush off** and reclaim loose silver dust so it doesn't get fired onto the plate. Don't wipe the silver design with alcohol or it will smear.

10 Clean stray silver from the plate with alcohol, avoiding the tree and lettering.

11 Fire according to the Ceramics With Overlay schedule. Let cool.

12 Use an agate burnisher to shine the silver **[J]**.

A family tree ornament uses a lot of silver but it's a beautiful keepsake.

> **Read more** about the parts of a gemstone and setting CZs on page 102.

5 Appendix

Gallery

We're sharing some of our favorite variations as inspiration for your next project.

Sgraffito piggy bank variation by Rob Stott

Patterns

For Family Tree project, p. 94

Enlarge or reduce to fit your project

For Celtic Charm project, p. 52

Firing Schedules

Follow the schedule for the type of clay you're using. Times listed are minimums; for the strongest possible silver, fire at the highest recommended temperature for *at least* the minimum time listed. See manufacturer's instructions for additional firing information.

LOW-FIRE

Clay	1110°F (600°C)	1200°F (650°C)	1290°F (700°C)	1380°F (750°C)	1472°F (800°C)	1562°F (850°C)	1600°F (870°C)	1650°F (900°C)	Torch	Stovetop	Shrinkage
ACS 650*	—	30 min.	15 min.	10 min.	5 min.	5 min.	5 min.	5 min.	yes	yes	8–9%
PMC3	45 min.	20 min.	10 min.	5 min.	5 min.	5 min.	5 min.	5 min.	yes	yes	10–12%
ACS 650 Slow-Dry	—	30 min.	15 min.	10 min.	5 min.	5 min.	5 min.	5 min.	yes	yes	8–9%
ACS Overlay Paste	—	30 min.	15 min.	10 min.	5 min.	5 min.	5 min.	5 min.	silver only	silver only	8–9%
ACS Standard	—	—	—	—	30 min.	20 min.	10 min.	10 min.	yes	yes	8–9%
Original PMC	—	—	—	—	—	—	—	2 hours	no	no	25–30%
PMC+	—	—	—	—	30 min.	20 min.	20 min.	10 min.	no	no	10–15%

Ceramics With Overlay: Ceramics must be heated and cooled very slowly to avoid thermal shock and breakage. Fire in kiln only. Ramp up at 500°F (260°F) per hour. Hold at 1200°F (650°C) for 30 minutes. Cool in kiln. Do not open kiln door until it reaches room temperature.

* Includes ACS 650 paste and syringe clays.

Birthstones

Month	Birthstone	Alternative	Color
January	Garnet	Rose quartz	Dark red
February	Amethyst	Onyx	Purple
March	Aquamarine	Bloodstone	Pale blue
April	Diamond	Rock crystal, white sapphire	White
May	Emerald	Chrysoprase	Bright green
June	Pearl	Moonstone, alexandrite	Cream
July	Ruby	Carnelian	Red
August	Peridot	Sardonyx	Pale green
September	Sapphire	Lapis lazuli	Deep blue
October	Opal	Tourmaline, zircon	Variegated
November	Topaz	Citrine	Yellow
December	Turquoise	Blue zircon, blue topaz	Sky blue

Gemstones and Silver Clay

Clay capture

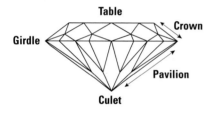

Syringe clay bezel

There are more than a few ways to set gemstones in silver clay, and the first indicator as to which type of setting you should use is the gemstone itself. There are two basic types of gemstones, as far as metal clay is concerned: fireable and nonfireable.

The safest gemstones to work with are cubic zirconia, commonly called CZs. These faux stones are created in a lab under extreme heat and pressure, forming in conditions similar to those inside a kiln. Created to mimic high-quality natural precious gemstones, CZs are inexpensive and come in a wide variety of shapes, colors, and sizes.

A few natural gemstones will tolerate kiln-firing, such as garnet, peridot, ruby, and sunstone. Any other natural stones must be added after firing.

If you're just starting out, we suggest that you stick to inexpensive and safe CZs. CZs, unlike natural stones, are perfect, which makes them better able to tolerate extremes of heating and cooling. Even so, a torch-fired CZ needs to be covered with a fiber blanket the instant it's fired and allowed to cool under the blanket. And never quench a stone of any kind—even a CZ!

Here are several easy ways of setting CZs in silver clay.

For a simple technique we call a clay capture, make a small hole in the clay where the gemstone will be placed. This hole helps vent the superhot air around the gemstone during firing and allows light to reflect through the back of the stone. With tweezers, place the stone upright in the hole. Press the stone into the clay until the *table*, the flat, top-most part of a faceted stone, is even with the top of the silver. The *culet*, the pointed bottom part, may stick out of the bottom of the silver; this is OK as long as the *girdle*, the widest part of the stone, is firmly trapped in the silver. If the girdle is firmly held, the stone cannot pop upward or downward out of the silver after firing. We used a clay capture in the tie tack project, p. 62.

Use a syringe clay bezel when the stone is deeper than the clay and you want to protect the culet of the stone. Make a hole for the stone in the clay and place three rings of syringe clay (more if the stone is extra deep) around the hole. Use tweezers to place the stone into the rings, and press on the stone with the tweezers until the table of the stone is even with the top of the rings. As the clay sinters, the silver will grasp the girdle of the stone tightly. We used syringe clay bezels in the birthstone bracelet project (p. 56) and the Family Tree project (p. 94).

Making Toggle Clasps

Toggle clasps are an attractive and personalized alternative to a purchased clasp, especially when you've worked so hard to make the rest of the bracelet or necklace yourself.

A toggle has two parts: a bar and a catch (often ring shaped). The catch is easily made using rolled clay, a texture stamp, and clay cutters in different sizes of the same shape.

Roll the clay to a minimum of 1.5 mm/ 6 cards. To create pattern on both sides, trap the clay between textures as you roll. Use the small cutter first and then center the larger cutter around the smaller shape [A, B].

You'll need a way to link the catch to the rest of the necklace or bracelet. You can bend the shank of a fine silver screw eye at a 90-degree angle and embed it in the clay before firing or attach a large jump ring around the catch after it's fired.

The toggle bar is even easier than the catch. Roll the clay just a bit thicker than the catch, and texture it in the same way. Trim the bar so that it's no more than ¼ the width of the catch and about ¼ longer [C, D]. With these proportions, the toggle bar should slip through the hole of the catch easily for wearing but will be large enough to hold securely while worn.

Trim the toggle bar to size, embed a bent screw eye into the wet clay [E], and use paste to reinforce the attachment. Dry the clay completely, smooth the edges with sanding paper or pads, and fire. The toggle is now ready to add personality to your latest piece!

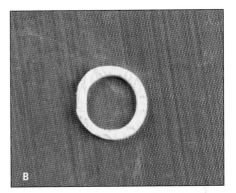

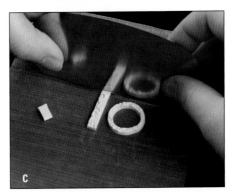

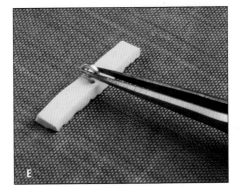

Toggle catches do not have to be round, mind you. Alternatives to the traditional round catch make a piece snappy and unique.

quick reference

MATERIALS & TOOLS
10 grams low-fire silver clay
Fine silver screw eye
Texture plate
Round cutters

TOOL KITS
Wet-clay tool kit
Finishing tool kit

Making Photopolymer Plates

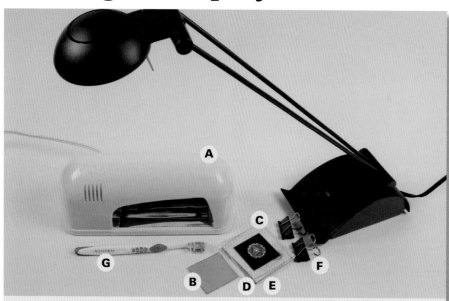

PLATEMAKING KIT

[A] nine-watt UV-cure lamp (or halogen lamp), [B] photopolymer plate, [C] printable transparency, [D] picture glass square, [E] opaque square (wood or cardboard) to fit design, [F] large binder clips, [G] soft toothbrush, access to printer or photocopier.

With photopolymer plates, you can create your own crisp, detailed, reusable stamps or textures of anything you can draw or photocopy in black and white.

We recommend easy-to-use photopolymer plates that cure in approximately 30 seconds under a UV or halogen lamp and are easily trimmed with scissors. Other photopolymer products are tin backed, requiring tin snips or metal-cutting tools, and require additional processing. (Our recommended photopolymer product is carried through many silver clay distributors, such as Art Clay World USA, Rings & Things, and Whole Lotta Whimsy.)

The items you'll need are easy to find and to use: a UV-cure lamp (recommended) or halogen lamp, an opaque square (such as wood or cardboard), a square of picture glass, a soft toothbrush, access to hot water, printable transparency film, and large binder clips. (The last two items can be found at any office supply store.) You can use the transparency film in a computer printer or in a photocopier. The photopolymer plates have a distinct smell, so work in a well-ventilated area if you find the scent objectionable.

The UV-cure lamp is the type you'd find in a nail salon; it has a 9-watt UV fluorescent bulb and will cure the photopolymer in about 30 seconds. A halogen lamp is perfectly usable but takes longer to cure—up to 8 minutes at a distance of 2 in. from the photopolymer. The opaque square prevents UV rays from penetrating te photopolymer plate and reflecting back up from the bottom, hardening areas that would otherwise not harden.

The transparency should be compatible with the type of printer you'll use; the printed transparency will be the negative for your texture plate. The picture glass provides a flat, clear surface that the UV rays can penetrate and that can be used as the top platform for the binder clips to hold the materials together during exposure. The opaque square and the glass need to be at least ⅛ in. (3 mm) larger than your design.

Creating the design

There are many copyright-free designs available via the internet or in books (see p. 107). Many people enjoy drawing their own textures and patterns; these can be scanned and printed, or simply photocopied, onto the transparency.

The white in your design will become the impressed area of your finished silver, and whatever is black will be raised.

This means that you should make the background of your image black—the opposite of what we're used to seeing. If you're working in photo-editing software, use the inverse function to transpose the black and white areas. Print or photocopy the inverted design to size onto the transparency film.

Work with photopolymer sheet in an area that does not have a lot of natural sunlight to minimize unwanted exposure to UV rays. Trim the photopolymer to fit the design dimensions, leaving approximately ⅛–¼ in. (3–7 mm) of blank photopolymer surrounding the image. Remove the top film from the photopolymer sheet [A].

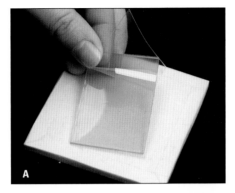

Place the photopolymer piece on top of the opaque square, then cover with the design transparency. If your design includes words, place the transparency over the photopolymer so that the script reads in reverse on the stamp. (When you stamp the clay, it will read correctly.) Cover the transparency with the clear glass square, and hold everything together with binder clips to ensure an even exposure [B]. The binder clips keep the layers from separating, preventing uneven exposure.

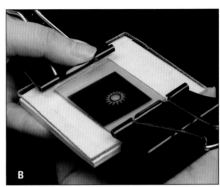

Place the photopolymer sandwich under a 9-watt UV-cure lamp for 25–30 seconds [C] (try 2–8 minutes if you're using a 50-watt halogen lamp). Halogen lamps are less predictable than UV-cure lamps. Unfortunately, there is no way to check to see if a design is set other than beginning to rinse the plate, and by then it is impossible to backtrack to earlier steps. But after one or two tests, you will begin to know how much time your UV lamp requires to set the photopolymer.

When the exposure time is up, rinse the plate in very warm water. (Don't put the photopolymer into boiling water; it will melt.) Use the toothbrush to brush away the still-soft areas of the photopolymer

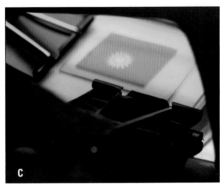

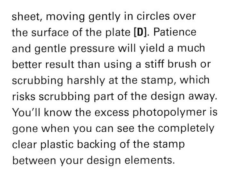

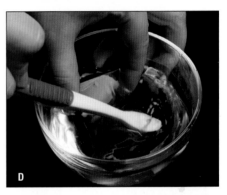

sheet, moving gently in circles over the surface of the plate [D]. Patience and gentle pressure will yield a much better result than using a stiff brush or scrubbing harshly at the stamp, which risks scrubbing part of the design away. You'll know the excess photopolymer is gone when you can see the completely clear plastic backing of the stamp between your design elements.

Dry the plate by blotting it with a sponge or blowing it with hot air from a hair dryer for a few moments. The plate will seem slightly sticky. Place the plate under the lamp again to finish curing. At this point, there is no danger of overexposure, so don't worry about how long it stays under the lamp. Once the tackiness is gone, the stamp is ready for use—and reuse. Trim any excess backing [E] and be sure to oil the stamp before use.

Adding Color

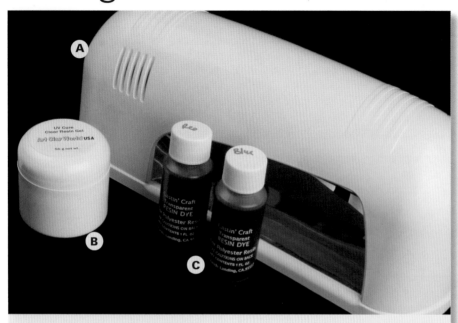

UV-CURE RESIN KIT
[A] UV-cure lamp or halogen lamp, [B] resin gel, and [C] dyes. Also needed (not shown): resin cleanser, toothpicks, glass square or glazed ceramic tile, long-necked butane lighter.

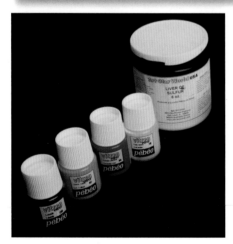

Pebeo Vitrea is simple to use, vibrant, and nontoxic.

Using UV Resin Gel
UV (ultraviolet) resin gel is a clear, viscous gel that remains liquid until exposed to UV rays. The same UV-cure lamp used to make photopolymer plates can be used to cure this resin. The gel has the thickness and consistency of honey and thins when heated. (Judi likes to heat the resin on a mug warmer to thin it for use; Katie prefers to leave it thick.) The resin is crystal clear but can be tinted with dyes, paints, and other media.

Plan ahead as you shape your silver clay piece, leaving depressions or texture in the silver that you can fill with resin after you fire it. Use toothpicks to draw the resin from its container. A little dye goes a long way, so put just a few drops of resin on a glass square or a glazed white ceramic tile (the glass or tile makes a great mixing palette) with just one or two drops of dye in the opposite corner. Use a toothpick to draw some of the dye into the resin, and mix until you have the color you want. Use the same toothpick to drop the resin onto the fired silver. (You'll need a new toothpick when changing colors or reaching back into the gel jar.)

If you see unwanted bubbles, use a long-necked butane lighter (usually used to light candles) to quickly heat the resin, thinning it so that air rises to the surface. Be careful not to singe any layer below the resin. Once you're bubble free, place the resin under a UV-cure lamp for about 2 minutes (a little longer if you used dark dye) or under a halogen lamp for up to 12 minutes. (See the resin project, p. 64, or the frame project, p. 67, for examples of using UV resin gel.)

Painting with Pebeo Vitrea
With Pebeo Vitrea, a brand of water-based paint designed for use on glass, you can easily add color to metal clay projects (see the piggy bank project, p. 82). Vitrea is dishwasher safe, so it is a good candidate for decorating wineglasses, tea or coffee mugs, or anything that will not be heated higher than 300°F (150°C).

As a decorative medium, Vitrea is also among the easiest to apply. Treat it as you would any other paint; colors can be mixed together and painted onto a surface with a paintbrush, and paintbrushes can be cleaned in plain water. Don't mix other types of paint with Vitrea. Paint the Vitrea onto a clean silver, glass, or stoneware surface, then allow it to dry for 24 hours. Once dry, place the item in your home oven at 300°F (150°C) for 35 minutes. The cured paint is food safe and dishwasher safe.

Published Resources

For images

Dover booklets are a great source for all kinds of copyright-free art. Many of the titles include a CD-ROM with the images. Here are some of our Dover favorites:
- *Trees and Leaves Electronic Clip Art*
- *Stencil Designs Clip Art Series*
- *Wild Animal Silhouettes Clip Art Series*
- *Art Nouveau Small Frames and Borders Clip Art Series*
- *Art Nouveau Frames and Borders*
- *Borders, Frames & Decorations of the Art Nouveau Period*
- *Butterfly Stained Glass Coloring Book*
- *159 Celtic Designs*

For those of you interested in the history and mythology of precious stones, including the lore of birthstones, we recommend *The Curious Lore of Precious Stones*. Another book we like for its cool kanji characters is *Kanji Pict-o-Graphix* by Michael Rowley (Stone Bridge Press). For the Family Tree project, *The Illustrated Encyclopedia of Trees* (Timber Press) is an awesome resource.

For additional silver clay information

Art Clay Silver & Gold by Jackie Truty (Krause)
Metal Clay, The Complete Guide by Jackie Truty (Krause)
Metal Clay Beyond the Basics by Carol A. Babineau (Kalmbach Books)

Downloadable resources

Art Clay Society, artclaysociety.com
Art Clay World USA, artclayworld.com
PMC Guild, pmcguild.com

Sources for Supplies, Tools, and More

Art Clay World USA
866-381-0100 or 708-857-8800
artclayworld.com

Brea Bead Works
714-671-9976
info@breabeadworks.com
breabeadworks.com

Cool Tools
888-478-5060
sales@cooltools.us
cooltools.us

Fire Mountain Gems
800-355-2137
questions@firemtn.com
firemountaingems.com

Maryland China Company
(great china for use with ACS Overlay Paste)
800-638-3880 or 410-833-5559
marylandchina.com

Metal Clay Supply
metalclaysupply.com
800-388-2001

Pearl Fine Art Supplies
800-451-7327
pearlpaint.com

Rings & Things
800-366-2156
rings-things.com

Rio Grande
800-545-6566
riogrande.com

Whole Lotta Whimsy
520-531-1966
staff@wholelottawhimsy.com
wholelottawhimsy.com

Glossary

Alloy Metallic material that is a blend of either two or more metals, or a metal and another element, usually to enhance a specific quality of the metal (e.g. to add strength, durability, etc.) Sterling silver is an alloy.

Applique The technique of taking pieces of one material and applying them to the surface of another.

Bail A loop or connective finding for the purpose of attaching a pendant or charm to a necklace or chain.

Beveled The angle of a surface that meets another at any angle but 90°.

Bezel The metal rim that holds a gemstone.

Binder In the case of metal clay, the organic substance that holds moist clay together. The binder burns away during firing.

Bone dry The stage where metal clay is completely free of moisture; test with method on p. 12.

Burnish To polish by friction or compression.

Cabochon A polished, domed gemstone without faceting.

Conditioning Lightly oiling a mold or texture plate to allow silver clay to release more easily; also the process of kneading a fresh piece of lump clay to soften it and prepare it for work.

Cubic zirconium (CZ) A synthetic stone available in many colors that has properties very similar to the properties of diamonds.

Emboss To press, carve or mold in relief, as in the design that is embossed on the face of a coin.

Embed To bury or affix firmly into.

Extrude To shape clay by forcing it through a tube.

Facets Symmetrical shapes or patterns that are cut into the surface of a crystal to enhance the transmission and reflection of light.

Filigree Fine, lacy ornament.

Findings Components of jewelry making, such as clasps, earring wires and backs, jump rings, pin backs, and hooks.

Fine silver 99.9% pure silver; what silver clay becomes after firing.

Finishing Techniques that put the final touches on a jewelry item; includes steps like sanding, polishing, tumbling, and adding a patina.

Firescale A reddish-purple discoloration that appears on silver/copper alloys (such as sterling silver) when they are heated in the presence of oxygen, whether through soldering or in a kiln.

Glazed ceramics Ceramics that are coated with glass-forming frit (ground glass) or minerals blended with assorted chemical components to produce color. Glazes can be produced in a variety of finishes—matte, semi-gloss, or high-gloss.

Greenware Dried, unfired clay items.

Grit The particulate grade in sandpaper that determines the abrasiveness of the sandpaper and the amount of material that will be removed from the piece being sanded. The larger the number, the finer the grit.

Inclusion A flaw in a natural gemstone that can appear as a feathering line, fissure, fracture, carbon spot, or cloud.

Inorganic Mineral- or petroleum-based substances, such as craft foam.

Lacquer A clear coating applied as a protective finish.

Leather hard The stage where metal clay is partially dry but still malleable.

Matte finish A soft, semi-reflective surface. Also called a "brushed finish."

Metal clay A clay-like creative medium used to make jewelry, beads, and small art objects, consisting of very small particles of silver, gold, or other metal mixed with an organic binder and water.

Mirror finish The most reflective surface that can be created on metal.

Mold A fabricated form into which another substance is pressed or poured to create a particular shape.

Natural gemstone A naturally occurring gem-quality crystal (as opposed to a synthetic or lab-created stone).

Organic A compound derived from living organisms or containing the compounds of carbon.

Patina A natural or induced reaction created on metal surfaces under the influences of air, water, earth, or certain chemicals. Liver of sulfur solution creates a patina for silver in vivid hues of gold, blue, copper, and purple.

Photopolymer Plate material that is used to make stamping images. It is photosensitive, and upon exposure to light, its compounds polymerize (harden like plastic) to form a tough, abrasion-resistant surface.

Polymer clay A modeling compound composed primarily of PVC resin, plasticizer, pigments, and other fillers that hardens in an oven.

Pre-finish To sand and smooth an item while it is in the dried, greenware state.

Quenching Rapidly cooling a heated silver item by dousing it in water; also called crash-cooling.

Ramp Increasing or decreasing kiln temperature at a programmed rate, such as 500°F (260°C) per hour.

Scribe To incise clay with needle tools, knives, or other sharp tools.

Sinter The process of fusing silver particles by heating them to a temperature just under their melting point.

Sgraffito From the Italian word for "scratched," sgraffito (as used in metal clay) is a decorative technique where the surface plating of Overlay Paste is scratched away to form a design.

Stamp To produce an imprint on clay with a flat mold or texture plate.

Sterling silver A standard jewelry-grade metal containing 925 parts silver and 75 parts of another metal, usually copper.

Tarnish A dulled luster or finish caused by a thin deposit of oxidation that discolors the surface of silver. Tarnish is easily removed with silver polish. Fine silver will tarnish more slowly than sterling silver.

Texture plate A sheet of plastic, rubber, metal, or other material that is impressed with a pattern. Used to transfer pattern to the surface of rolled metal clay.

Ultraviolet (UV) The invisible rays of the spectrum of light at its violet end. UV light is used to set certain types of resins, causing them to change from a viscous liquid to a clear, solid form.

Viscous A liquid or gas with a relatively thick, dense consistency. Honey is a viscous liquid, as is UV resin.

Wet clay Clay that is completely moist and malleable.

About the Authors

Katie (left) and Judi with Josie, one of three pooches that own the two authors

Katie Baum

Katie began her teaching career in 2003 as a middle-school science teacher. She has always been fascinated with sciences and experimentation, initially approaching silver clay with a logical "How is this possible?" attitude before falling in love with its versatility and creative possibilities. Katie came to work full-time with Art Clay World USA headquarters in mid-2007 after earning her Art Clay Senior Instructor status from Art Clay Senior Instructor and long-time mentor Judi Hendricks. Katie was initially certified by Jackie Truty, an Art Clay Master Instructor and president of Art Clay World USA.

Katie's focus and passion have always been teaching, and metal clay has provided a perfect combination of teaching/ learning opportunity with the ability to artistically release and imaginatively nurture her soul. Since beginning her position as the director of the Art Clay Society in 2007, Katie has traveled to teach, speak, or participate in over a dozen conferences, studio events, and trade shows—with many more to come.

In addition to directing the Art Clay Society, maintaining its Web site, and publishing its newsletters, Katie is also the marketing and advertising director and the wholesale accounts manager with Art Clay World USA. In her "spare time," Katie hopes to converse more often with her muses and create pieces from her heart and spirit.

Judi L. Hendricks

Judi sees life as a never-ending journey of creative expression and so is accustomed to starting off in one direction and ending up somewhere completely unexpected or going in five directions at once. In her daily life, she's a contract designer whose projects range from developing data collection tools for the pharmaceutical research industry to designing print ads. In her evening and weekend lives, she's a clairvoyant counselor, teaching meditation, psychic awareness, and energy healing; a garden designer; a silver clay artist and teacher; and dog mother. She's also a potter, combining her work in porcelain clay with Art Clay Overlay Paste to create new levels of expression. Of her pottery, she says, "I love shaping the earth. It's like playing with mud where you just might end up with a cereal bowl."

A psychology major in college, Judi abandoned this discipline to pursue ordination as an interfaith minister. She believes that "psychotherapy doesn't heal people—people heal themselves as they regain balance with their creative purpose and relationship to the Divine."

Judi feels that everyone has an inner artist. "I feel that souls were born to create," she says. She believes that a lot of pain that people experience occurs when they have lost touch with their creative spark and creative process, almost as though they have forgotten how to enjoy playing, which makes it hard to enjoy life. Part of Judi's ministry is to help people express whatever it is they are meant to create. She believes that silver clay's ultra-fast learning curve and affordability makes it a perfect playful medium for reopening the door to personal creative expression.

Acknowledgments

With two authors, there is no shortage of folks who deserve our gratitude and appreciation. Deep thanks to the staff at Art Clay World USA—particularly Jackie and Tom Truty—for their patience, understanding, and support as Katie took the time to focus on this book, not to mention their contribution of resources and materials.

Immeasurable thanks to David Baum, our project-in-progress photographer, for working with us these long hours and long drives through never-ending roadway construction. His dedication and humor were perfect for this silvery undertaking.

We would like to give due recognition and merit to Robert Stotts of MonkeyHaüs Design for his design contributions, from piggy banks to trinket boxes. We decorated some of Rob's pottery with silver for projects, including the dog treat canister. Rob also provided the gallery photographs.

Credit is due to Neil Estrick for donating some of his exquisite pottery to our cause.

Thanks are in order, also, to Aida Chemical Industries, for supplying the product that Katie and Judi have fallen in love with and immersed themselves in.

Thanks to Mary Wohlgemuth at Kalmbach Books, for her support and guidance as this book came together, and for her wonderful handling of our barrage of questions and concerns.

Thanks to the artists and enthusiasts who—knowingly or not—contributed to the ideas, designs, and projects found within this book, with their questions, commissions, and wild silver clay fantasies.

And lastly, but most importantly, thanks to our husbands, who put up with our long hours, crazy demands, and emotions as we found our way in this project. Katie needs to thank her husband, Earl, for not just picking up her frazzled, raw pieces, but knowing just how to put them together and soothe everything into connectivity. Without Earl's strong support and gentle encouragement, Katie would not have had the courage to propose this project, and it is through his unwavering faith in her that she has completed this project and still retained some semblance of sanity. Katie dedicates her part in this book to Earl, the purest and shiniest part of her life. Judi would like to thank Rob for being a beacon of creativity and inspiration. She never ceases to be amazed at the beautiful things that flow from his hands and into the world.

Put your creativity to work
with inspirational projects

Hip Handmade Memory Jewelry
With easy-to-make projects using simple craft materials and beading supplies, this book shows you how to turn photos and other mementos into cool, wearable necklaces, earrings, bracelets, and more.
62748 • $21.95

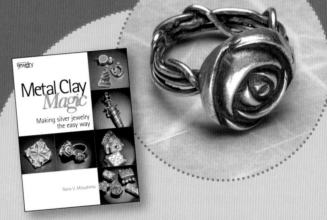

Metal Clay Magic
This volume includes more than 25 step-by-step projects with instructions for rolling, stamping, finishing and combining metal clay with other materials.
62202 • $21.95

Silver Threads
Packed with dazzling full-color photos, this book features detailed, illustrated instructions for 12 stunning projects that range from simple pendants to more complex necklaces.
62210 • $22.95

Available at your favorite bead or craft shop!

KB KALMBACH BOOK

Order online at
www.KalmbachBooks.com
or call 1-800-533-6644

Monday – Friday, 8:30 a.m. – 5:00 p.m. Central Standard Time.
Outside the U.S. and Canada call 262-796-8776, ext. 661.